THE
FAST SET

Edwardian Goodwood

GEORGE PLUMPTRE

THE
FAST SET

The World of Edwardian Racing

ANDRE DEUTSCH

By the same author

ROYAL GARDENS

COLLINS BOOK OF BRITISH GARDENS

First published 1985 by
André Deutsch Limited
105 Great Russell Street London WC1

ISBN 0 233 97754 6

Printed in Great Britain by
R. J. Acford Limited, Chichester, Sussex

For Rara

*Royal victories were universally popular and
provided a rich trade in mementos.*

CONTENTS

ACKNOWLEDGEMENTS

My primary thanks are to Lord Howard de Walden for writing a Foreword to the book. I cannot pretend that when I originally approached him I knew that he was going to achieve a lifelong ambition by winning the Derby with Slip Anchor. But it seems fitting that the book is being published in the same year as his triumph.

There are also a number of other people I would like to thank for their help or advice during the book's research and production: Lord Londonderry, Hugh McCalmont, Hugh Montgomery-Massingberd, Roger Mortimer, Richard Onslow, Michael Oswald, Lord Porchester, Lord Savile, Guy Wilmot, the staff of the National Horseracing Museum, and, in particular, Henry Plumptre.

Finally my thanks to Caroline Knox – who originally suggested the book – and Sara Menguc at André Deutsch, and my agent Vivienne Schuster.

PHOTOGRAPHIC ACKNOWLEDGEMENTS

Her Majesty the Queen: 57; BBC Hulton Picture Library: 31, 33, 42a&b, 62b, 74a&b, 81, 89, 92, 128b, 132, 135, 150, 152, 153, 161, 168b; Christopher Sykes: 59, 62c, 77, 83; Illustrated London News: 170, 172; Lord Londonderry: 34, 97b; Mary Evans Picture Library: 85; National Horseracing Museum: 4, 23a, 118b, 121, 123, 160; National Portrait Gallery: 46; Richard Onslow: 101a; Racing Illustrated: 19, 23b, 24, 25a, 30b, 48, 49, 53, 56, 61, 62a, 66, 67, 69, 70, 71, 74c, 80, 82, 88, 101b, 104, 110, 116, 145; W. W. Rouch and Co: 25b, 27, 44, 51, 54a&b, 59b, 112, 115, 118a, 127, 128a, 130a, 139, 147, 155, 157, 163, 165b&c, 168a; The Royal Photographic Society: 2, 13, 15a&b&c, 16, 17, 30a, 37, 107, 137, 141a&b, 143a&b&c&d, 149a&b, 159, 165a; Trustees of the British Library: 91; Trustees of the Goodwood Collection: 12, 41, 167.

FOREWORD

This book covers the most glamorous period of racing and a period when the people involved, whether they were big owners, trainers, jockeys, or even money lenders, seem larger than life.

I am fortunate to be old enough to have a very tenuous connection with some of the characters who stride through these pages.

When I was at a preparatory school my Mother took me for some reason or other to Cannes. I think she had something special to do one afternoon and handed me over to Sir Hugo de Bathe, known as 'Sugie', who was about to order some clothes.

I can well remember that afternoon with Lily Langtry's husband and his very perfect sartorial requirements.

A little later I was allowed to go to Newmarket to see one of my Father's horses run and my Father, for some inexplicable reason, put me in a train under the auspices of Bob Siever (the famous, or infamous, owner and trainer of Sceptre). My Father had a soft spot for Bob Siever, from whom in later years he used to buy bull terriers.

I remember my Father telling me that whatever may have been said about Bob Siever, and a lot was said to his detriment, that he never ran his horses dishonestly.

These pages are full of the atmosphere of those days and the camaraderie that seems to have existed between the social stratas all preoccupied with the racing and gambling world.

I feel that it is rather sad that apart from Her Majesty The Queen nobody high in Government seems to take an interest in what is our oldest national sport, and now a worldwide business as well, that was started in this country. Sir Winston Churchill is the last Prime Minister to have been an owner, although Sir Alec Douglas-Home, when Prime Minister, is reputed to have had a bet or two every day!

Nowadays a more puritan outlook prevails and there is an idea that racing is raffish and not quite honest.

I hope those who read these pages will realize that racing was, and still

can be, fun for a large number of people and personally I hope that the day will come when those in high places will realize that racing should be considered part of our national heritage, just as much as large houses and paintings.

Lord Howard de Walden

INTRODUCTION

*King Edward VII as Prince of Wales at the turn of the century: the decisive
figure in racing's increasing social importance.*

In 1875 three seemingly unconnected events took place. A horse called Galopin
won the Derby. The Prince of Wales (later King Edward VII) registered his
racing colours: 'purple, gold braid, scarlet sleeves, black velvet cap with gold
fringe'. And Sandown Park became the first course in England with a
members' enclosure, limited to proposed and seconded members. Together
they heralded a golden age of racing which was to last for the next four
decades. Galopin went on to sire St Simon, the greatest horse of the nineteenth
century. The Prince's patronage invested racing with a new social importance,
which reached a peak in the early years of the twentieth century. The members'
enclosures enabled Society to attend race meetings in civilized comfort away
from the less desirable members of the racing public.

No other pastime appealed to the Edwardians quite so much as racing.
With plenty of money and more than enough time for leisure, they found
the excitement and glamour of the sport irresistable. They patronized it with
vigour and, at times, huge extravagance, spending fortunes – whether they
could afford to do so or not – on buying and breeding horses, building studs
and training stables, on lavish house parties for race meetings and, not least,

on gambling. More money was spent and lost with the bookmakers during a single season than was available in prize-money during the whole period.

The sums involved were often enormous. Between 1875 and 1914 the average value of the pound was thirty-five times greater than today; thus a single bet of £10,000 – not a rarity – was the equivalent of £350,000. Similarly, when a big spender such as George Alexander Baird squandered around £2 million in just over ten years he was spending, in today's terms, in the region of £70 million.

The appeal was both competitive and social. The great aristocratic owners such as the Dukes of Westminster and Portland were primarily interested in breeding and owning the best horses of the day. They combined rare knowledge with vast financial assets to achieve spectacular results. To many others racing was the means to an end. Alfred de Rothschild, one of the richest and most colourful characters of the period, once remarked that the finest

The Duke of Richmond's house party for Goodwood 1906 – the first year that Edward VII decreed that it was permissible not to wear a frock coat and top hat. The King's mistress, Alice Keppel, is seated at a discreet distance from His Majesty on the extreme left, while the Marchioness of Londonderry reclines with characteristic grandeur second from the right.

publicity a man could buy himself was a racehorse. When Lieutenant-General Sir Reginald Pole-Carew was asked by the Duke of Portland why he had bought a mare, having shown no previous interest in racing, 'Polly' replied: 'My dear fellow, I think every gentleman should own a thoroughbred mare.'

What had previously been the indulgence of a few sporting aristocrats and magnates – not to mention the livelihood of a frightening array of vagabonds and criminals – became, by the end of the century, a national pastime. More important, it became the playground of Society. Select race meetings – the Derby and Oaks at Epsom, Royal Ascot, the Newmarket and Goodwood summer meetings and the St Leger at Doncaster – became major events in the social calendar. The transformation was quite dramatic, as revealed by Lady Augusta Fane, who wrote in her memoirs that, 'In those days [the early 1870s] racing was not considered a sport suitable for young ladies . . . of course an exception was made for Ascot.' Even so, on her first visit to Ascot there were not more than one hundred women in the Royal Enclosure and when her mother had attended in 1858 there were perhaps fifteen or twenty. By the turn of the century there would be thousands.

It was hardly surprising that racing was not considered suitable for young ladies. Before the safety of a members' enclosure was introduced they were extremely vulnerable. Disraeli once described a Derby Day crowd as, 'a quarter of a million, including all the ruffianism that London and every

Looking across the course to Epsom Downs on Derby Day; a national festival throughout the Edwardian era.

racecourse in the kingdom can produce.' Physical assault may have become less of a hazard than it had been earlier in the century, but verbal abuse and pickpockets were commonplace. In most instances the assailants were quite unabashed, regarding the racing 'swells' as fair game. When Sir George Chetwynd's tie-pin was stolen at Newmarket, he complained to the Earl of Lonsdale, knowing that 'the Sporting Earl' enjoyed a nodding acquaintance with a selection of the rogues who frequented the racecourse. In time the pin was returned – by an individual dressed up as a vicar – at the cost of £25 to Sir George. Even worse, as he was leaving the races, Sir George was accosted by a scruffy-looking boy who demanded to know how much he had paid for the pin's return. On hearing the sum the urchin exclaimed with disgust, 'Blimey! Twenty-five nicker. 'E only gave me ten bob and I stole the bloody thing.'

Not only were racecourses unsafe; to mid-Victorian society the sport appeared to be little more than a succession of unsavoury scandals. Normally their repercussions did not spread beyond the racing fraternity, but when they did they were received with widespread horror. It seemed that racing was synonymous with excessive gambling, heavy drinking, womanizing and a generally immoral existence, especially among younger members of the aristocracy, some of whom managed to ruin themselves before they had the chance to enjoy their inheritance.

Victorian society in general disapproved of the raffish and reckless patrons of the Turf, but there was one person who took an especially dim view of the goings-on – Queen Victoria. In the years after her marriage the young Queen had enjoyed attending Royal Ascot. On the death of her beloved Prince Albert her visits stopped abruptly. Although she gave up attending, the Queen's involvement in racing continued indirectly and during her reign the royal stud at Hampton Court produced the winners of eight Classics. Her worst fears were focused on her son, Albert Edward, Prince of Wales, who was showing disturbing signs of thoroughly enjoying life among people his mother considered to be dubious or disreputable. Despite all her efforts, however, it was to prove one of the few confrontations with his mother which Bertie won conclusively.

The Prince's patronage gave racing the supreme accolade. In his position as the acknowledged head of Society he gave a lead to those around him which was followed with enthusiasm. As the Jockey Club began to exert a controlling influence and race meetings became safer, more enjoyable and more accessible, so the royal impetus made racing socially *de rigeur*. Friendship with the Prince of Wales was the best guarantee of social success. At the same

The fortune teller: a regular feature of Derby Day.

Refreshment on the Downs at the Derby.

All eyes on the King (and his companion) in the Royal Box at Ascot.

Society at leisure. Royal Ascot, 1910.

time men like Sir Blundell Maple, the furniture magnate, Baron de Hirsch, the Jewish industrialist and Jack and Solly Joel, the Jewish diamond kings, proved that spending their fortunes on racing was a certain passport to social elevation.

In striking contrast to previous decades, as racing became more social it became a pastime for the ladies. Although it was unacceptable for them to own their own horses, women were expected to be able to talk about racing. It was as important to look good on a horse as it was to be good-looking – if anything, the former quality drew more widespread admiration. Catherine Walters, better known as 'Skittles' and the most renowned courtesan at the beginning of the period, aroused furious jealousy among many women but could be forgiven anything by most men because, when mounted on a horse, her appearance was incomparable.

The ladies also played leading roles in the house parties which became an integral part of life off-course. Competition among hostesses to give the largest and smartest parties and to entertain the most important people was intense. The Prince of Wales was the greatest catch and a royal visit, however expensive, was considered a social triumph. Only occasionally did it lead to

disaster – as for the poor Wilson family who were ruined by the baccarat scandal which erupted at their home, Tranby Croft, during a house party for the St Leger in 1890.

Disasters of the magnitude of Tranby Croft were rare because by and large the Edwardians took care to keep their private lives out of the headlines. House parties provided the perfect opportunities for the affairs and liaisons which, by the turn of the century, had become quite acceptable, not only because of the proximity of bedrooms an accommodating hostess could normally be relied upon to provide, but also because of the privacy. A servant was far more likely to be dismissed for 'spilling the beans' than for some domestic error such as dropping the soup at dinner.

Many of the leading owners built up racing establishments on a similar scale to the hospitality they dispensed in their huge homes. At Eaton, Welbeck and Mentmore, the respective homes of the Duke of Westminster, the Duke of Portland and the Earl of Rosebery, the stables were almost as extensive as the houses. Racing had always had its grandees but never before had they indulged in quite such style – nor, after the First World War, were they to do so again. Racing as developed and enjoyed by the Edwardians achieved its peak of patronage by the rich and aristocratic. For a few decades it became as much a social occasion as a sporting event.

On display at Royal Ascot.

REFORM AND RESPECTABILITY

Unlike their predecessors, the society circulating round the Prince of Wales relished the dramas and scandals that were part and parcel of the Turf. Much of racing's corruption was, however, being stamped out. By the 1870s there had been considerable improvements and advances; in administration, in the growing authority of the Jockey Club and in the general cleaning up of the sport, on and off the course.

Before the 1870s the possibility for dishonesty, corruption or blatant crime existed in many aspects of racing and realistically there was no one with sufficient authority to oppose it. The total lack of any control over the type of people attending race meetings was one problem. A more serious threat was the potential for corruption among jockeys, stable staff and racing officials. Jockeys could deliberately 'pull' horses to prevent them winning when favourite to do so, thereby ensuring that they, their friends and the horse's owner would later win a substantial bet at long odds. Stable lads could advise on and assist in the poisoning or laming of horses (collectively known as 'nobbling'). Among racing officials, who were few and far between in these earliest days of organized racing, the most vulnerable were the handicappers, who decided the weights carried by horses. Besides a handful of the leading races such as the five Classics: the One Thousand and the Two Thousand Guineas, the Derby, the Oaks and the St Leger, which were competed for by horses of the same age carrying level weights, most races were run as handicaps, when horses carried different weights determined by their age and previous form. The possibilities for bending the rules – by paying off handicappers or by running a horse in a handicap with no intention of winning, so that the horse was given a low weight for its next race – were widespread. They were openly exploited to set up massive betting coups. Successful gambling, rather than ownership of outstanding horses, was the aim of many men involved in racing. Partly as a result of the unreliability of handicapping, many of the leading owners, who were primarily interested in their horses rather than gambling, avoided handicap races and preferred to run their horses in private matches. These were agreed privately by two owners, each of whom ran one horse. They were handicapped but there was not the potential for dishonesty

which existed in a public race. Much of the form for the Classics and other major races was established by these matches.

One man, the Honourable Admiral Henry Rous, a younger son of the Earl of Stradbroke, did more than any other to improve the rules and administration of racing. The redoubtable Admiral attacked his task with the crusading zeal of many of his contemporary social reformers. Strict, fair-minded and forthright, he was also fully aware of the problems he faced. In his book, *The Laws and Practice of Horseracing*, he wrote: 'Every great handicap offers a premium for fraud, for horses are constantly started without any intention of winning, merely to hoodwink the handicapper.' When the suggestion was first made to appoint a public handicapper, Rous argued that it would be impossible to find a man capable of fulfilling the task. This did not stop him accepting the job when it was pressed upon him by his fellow members of the Jockey Club.

Admiral Rous: Dictator of the Turf and wizard of handicapping.

Rous's unceasing attention to horses' form, at all major race meetings and at exercise, was legendary. Most mornings he was on the Heath at Newmarket – where there was the greatest concentration of horses – well before the trainers and their strings, field-glasses and notebook at the ready. During Newmarket races he sat motionless on his horse, concealed behind the bushes halfway along the course. Jockeys were a breed he disliked and mistrusted to a man and woe betide anyone who gave the impression of not

trying. The bellows of abuse which the Admiral poured on them could be heard way off at the finish. At other courses he watched from the top of the stand with the aid of a powerful telescope dating from his naval days. His dedication enabled him to evolve a system of handicapping which, while not completely foolproof, was certainly a radical improvement on anything which had gone before. Certainly few men could ever claim to have hoodwinked the Admiral. A few days before his death in 1877 the old man remarked, 'It's a very odd thing, I lose my way now going from the Turf Club (then in Grafton Street) to my house in Berkeley Square, but,' he added with satisfaction, 'I can still handicap.'

Age.	Mar. and April.	May.	June.	July.	Aug.	Sept.	Oct. and Nov.
	st. lb.	st. lb.	st. lb.	st. lb.	st. lb.	st. lb.	st. lb.
Five Furlongs.							
Two years	6 0	6 2	6 7	6 9	7 0	7 4	7 7
Three years	8 2	8 3	8 5	8 7	8 9	8 10	8 11
Four years	9 0	9 0	9 0	9 0	9 0	9 0	9 0
Five, six, and aged . .	9 1	9 0	9 0	9 0	9 0	9 0	9 0
Six Furlongs.							
Two years	6 0	6 4	6 7	6 11	7 0	7 5	7 7
Three years	8 4	8 6	8 8	8 10	8 12	9 0	9 2
Four years	9 7	9 7	9 7	9 7	9 7	9 7	9 7
Five, six, and aged . .	9 9	9 8	9 7	9 7	9 7	9 7	9 7
One Mile.							
Two years	—	—	—	—	—	6 5	6 7
Three years	7 9	7 11	7 13	8 2	8 4	8 5	8 6
Four years	9 0	9 0	9 0	9 0	9 0	9 0	9 0
Five, six, and aged . .	9 4	9 3	9 2	9 0	9 0	9 0	9 0
One Mile and a Half.							
Two years	—	—	—	—	—	6 0	6 4
Three years	7 7	7 9	7 11	7 13	8 1	8 3	8 5
Four years	9 0	9 0	9 0	9 0	9 0	9 0	9 0
Five, six, and aged . .	9 5	9 4	9 3	9 2	9 1	9 0	9 0
Two Miles.							
Two years	—	—	—	—	—	6 0	6 2
Three years	7 8	7 11	7 12	8 0	8 3	8 4	8 5
Four years	9 4	9 4	9 4	9 4	9 4	9 4	9 4
Five, six, and aged . .	9 10	9 9	9 8	9 7	9 6	9 5	9 4
Three Miles.							
Three years	7 1	7 4	7 5	7 7	7 9	7 11	7 13
Four years	9 0	9 0	9 0	9 0	9 0	9 0	9 0
Five years	9 8	9 7	9 6	9 5	9 5	9 4	9 3
Six and aged . . .	9 10	9 8	9 7	9 6	9 5	9 4	9 3

The scale of weight for age published by the Jockey Club at the turn of the century. It is based entirely on the scale drawn up by Admiral Rous in the 1870s, which provided the foundations of effective handicapping.

The improvement in handicapping was not the only aspect of racing about which the Admiral felt strongly. He deplored heavy betting and loathed aristocratic spendthrifts like the Marquess of Hastings. During the middle of the nineteenth century one of the most successful and richest owners was Sir Joseph Hawley. 'The Lucky Baronet', as he was known, owned four Derby winners. He was also an enthusiastic advocate of racing reform, but the uncompromising Admiral opposed all his efforts on principle because of Sir Joseph's heavy betting. He did, however, appreciate that betting was to an extent the lifeblood of racing. 'Suppress betting by legal enactment and the game is up; thoroughbred stock would depreciate sixty per cent and our racecourses would be ploughed up. Racing has always been and will always be, a gambling speculation.'

For just over twenty years the Admiral ruled racing and became, after Sir Charles Bunbury (at the end of the eighteenth century) and Lord George Bentinck (during the 1840s), the last of the three great Dictators of the Turf. His outspoken style made him many enemies and his career was punctuated by frequent and often abusive outbursts in letters to *The Times*. One such led the Day family, long established in training, but at the time unquestionably involved in some corrupt practice, to sue him for libel and the Admiral had to eat humble pie. His influence was, however, undeniable as he could be relied upon to settle any dispute or question with absolute authority, knowledge of the facts and impartiality. Fred Swindell, despite his name one of the few honest bookmakers during the Admiral's time, bought a house next to the great man in Berkeley Square to see who visited him. 'Lord Freddy' had started life as an engine-cleaner in Derbyshire. Fed up, he walked to London to make his fortune in racing. It is uncertain how much his proximity to the Admiral had to do with his success, but when he died Swindell left over £700,000.

It was largely thanks to Rous's efforts that, by the 1870s, the authority of the Jockey Club was becoming absolute. This élite group of aristocratic Turf magnates had had nominal power over most areas of racing for decades, but more often than not had been unable to impose their will. In 1870 *The Rules Concerning Horse Racing in General*, drawn up by the Jockey Club, were re-examined by the Club's three recently appointed stewards. When they were published it was clear that the Club had become confident of their power. A clear distinction was made between race meetings run under the Jockey Club rules and those that were 'unrecognized'. The Club ruled against publishing either the programmes or the results of the latter meetings in an attempt to stamp them out. They strengthened their position by adding that any trainer,

jockey or official who took part in an 'unrecognized' meeting would be penalized. Finally, the last quarter of the nineteenth century saw the successful application of a licence system by the Jockey Club. Trainers, jockeys, officials and indeed, racecourses, had to obtain a licence. Forfeit for any sort of misconduct normally meant 'warning off' for people and closure for courses.

The rules of 1870 clearly revealed the invaluable hand of Admiral Rous and his command of every aspect of racing. They fixed calendar limits for the flat season (25 March until 15 November), applied restrictions to the racing of two-year-olds and made five furlongs the minimum distance of a race. (This latter ruling was to stop the very short 'dashes' which had become popular and which were both an unrealistic test of a horse and probably harmful.) The Jockey Club also impressed upon the stewards appointed for various race meetings around the country the importance of using to the full their considerably extended powers, which included the ability to warn off a jockey on the spot for blatant misconduct. It had taken a very long time, but at last the Jockey Club was able to wield power to some effect. A few years before the rules were re-issued the Club showed their self-assurance when a bill was presented to Parliament concerning the minimum weight horses should carry. In a firmly worded message the Jockey Club made it quite clear that it felt rulings about racing to be none of Parliament's business and that they had no right to debate bills on the subject. The bill was withdrawn.

In 1876 the Club again redrafted the rules under a new title, which left no one in any doubt about their authority: *The Rules of Racing, as made by the Jockey Club at Newmarket*. Divided into nine parts, the rules had fifty-six clauses covering all aspects of racing. This code established ruling on the conduct of those involved in racing, on the limitations concerning the entering of horses for certain races, on the sums and payment of prize-money and all other relevant subjects, and the Jockey Club were able to spend the rest of the nineteenth century ensuring that it was effectively enforced.

The Jockey Club had gained not only administrative authority but territorial power. After Admiral Rous became Treasurer of the Club and reorganized and improved their finances, they had steadily bought up areas of Newmarket Heath from the private individuals who originally owned various sections. As a result they were able to apply their rules to the area which had by far the largest concentration of horses in training in the country. Their control extended to Newmarket racecourse and it was the rules established here which were soon imposed on other courses. One of the most important effects of this growing authority over racecourses was the decline of the previously mentioned 'unrecognized' racecourses. Most of these had

The Jockey Club's book of racing colours showing, top right, the Duke of Westminster's famous black and gold silks.

Newmarket High Street in the 1890s.

sprung up in the suburbs of London. Often opened on a speculative basis by private individuals, little or no attempt was made to bring any order to these proceedings. As a result they attracted exactly the kind of crooked jockeys and trainers, swindling bookmakers and out-and-out criminals that the Jockey Club was so eager to banish from the racing scene altogether. At the same time they were unsafe for any respectable race-goer. Added to the Jockey Club's efforts, the death knell for these last outposts of disreputable racing was Mr Anderson's Metropolitan Racecourse Bill of 1879, which banned all race meetings within a certain vicinity of the centre of London.

In their place came the park courses, far fewer in number, and set up along well organized lines with Jockey Club approval. Sandown Park was established by General Owen Williams, a member of the Jockey Club, on whose land the course was built. The General set up a company to finance the building and running of the new course and his brother, Hwfa Williams,

The parade for the Eclipse at Sandown: the first race to be worth £10,000.

General Owen Williams, on whose land Sandown Park was built.

Gatwick: one of the most popular suburban courses which has subsequently disappeared.

was Clerk of the Course for fifty years. Kempton Park was established by S.H. Hyde who, with other members of his family, had been actively involved in racing for some years. In 1872 Mr Hyde was driving from Hampton Court towards Sunbury when he came upon a stretch of outstanding parkland with a sign: 'Land for Sale or Lease'. Having set up a company to buy the four hundred-acre site he was able to open Kempton Park in 1878.

The organization of the park courses, which included charging an entrance fee and the establishment of different enclosures with varying prices, was aimed at encouraging the respectable race-goer, who in the past had been frightened off by the sort of person they were likely to come up against at any of the old suburban courses.

The success of these new courses partly resulted from the new enthusiasm among members of the public to pay for a day's racing in enjoyable surroundings. There was a steady expansion in the quantity and quality of good races, encouraged by both the new courses, the improvement of facilities at the major old ones and the administrative reforms by the Jockey Club. In 1843 the total prize-money in the season had been £198,990. By 1874 it had almost doubled to £315,272 and the sum continued to rise steadily for the rest of the century. Equally significant was the announcement by the management of Sandown Park in 1886 – eleven years after they had opened

the course – that they were to inaugurate the Eclipse Stakes, the first race in Britain ever to carry a stake of £10,000. The adventurous move was shown to be an instant success by the quality of the horses entered for the race. Run in July, the Eclipse has enjoyed virtual Classic status ever since. In his memoirs the Duke of Portland, a member of the Jockey Club and one of the leading owners of the last quarter of the nineteenth century, wrote:

> 'Towards the end of the '70s the park courses were opened. Sandown leading the way, followed by Kempton, Hurst Park and others. These, no doubt, much improved the status of the sport in many ways. In the days to which I allude, save for the so-called Classic Races, there were very few stakes to the value of one thousand sovereigns; and those that were, were all subscribed by the owners themselves with little or no added money given.'

The one area in which the Jockey Club refused to contemplate change was any attempt to diminish its oligarchical exclusivity. Something of a breakthrough was made when Baron Meyer de Rothschild was elected as the first Jewish member of the Club, but otherwise membership was limited to a select circle of aristocrats and landed gentry who positions were founded on old-established estates. Almost all held titles, or were closely related to families who did. In 1898 forty-one out of the fifty-four members held titles. In addition, there were eight members of the English and continental royal families, headed by the Prince of Wales, and a number of honorary members – mainly continental noblemen.

The influence of the Club at various racecourses was assisted by the fact that its members were among the most prominent figures in different parts of the country. More important was the authority it gained from the active involvement of a minority of members in national politics, such as the Duke of Devonshire and the Earl of Rosebery.

There is no doubt that the effective establishment of the Jockey Club's authority and their application of a workable set of rules for racing, led to the majority of the improvements in the sport. At the same time a revolution was brought about in the transport of horses by the advent of the railways. The result was an immediate expansion in the number of runners up and down the country: between 1837 and 1869 the number doubled, and continued to rise steadily through the rest of the century. Before the railways horses had to be walked to courses. Not only did this severely limit the number of meetings they could attend, it also meant that they might have to cover a distance of well over one hundred miles to run in one of the Classics. During the 1830s Lord George Bentinck transported his horse Elis from Goodwood

to Doncaster in a huge box drawn by six horses and brought off an unexpected victory in the St Leger, but the cumbersome prototype horse-box did not enjoy widespread popularity. By the last quarter of the nineteenth century the various networks of railways provided cheap, fast transport for horses and linked the training centres and racecourses in a way which a few decades earlier would never have seemed possible. One of the few disasters occurred in 1861, when a train from King's Cross to Malton in Yorkshire caught fire. In one of the vans was a horse called Klarikoff, who had been third in the Two Thousand Guineas and fifth in the Derby. His career came to an untimely end when he was burnt alive.

The advent of the railways was not the only improvement in communications from which racing benefitted. At the beginning of the 1870s it was not uncommon for results to be delivered by carrier pigeons. In 1896, when the Prince of Wales's Persimmon won the Derby, the race was the subject of the first publicly released newsreel.

The advent of the railways revolutionized the transportation of horses. Some took to it more readily than others.

Encouraged by the various improvements and reforms the leading owners responded with enthusiasm. It would be safe to say that a greater number of the most important horses in racing history were bred, raced and in their turn bred offspring during this period than at any other time. With the incentives of increased prize-money and more plentiful quality races the desire to breed and train outstanding horses grew rapidly. Improvements in breeding and training went hand-in-hand. During the middle decades of the nineteenth century horses were still 'sweated' and 'purged'. After being allowed to become overweight in the winter they were brought back into training by sweating – when they literally had a sauna, covered in rugs with a hot stove in their stable – and by purging, when they were given long hard gallops with heavy clothes on.

By the turn of the century these practices had long since disappeared. Many of the improvements, such as cooler and better ventilated stables, were introduced from America. In addition, horses were not worked as hard immediately before a race as they had been in the past, in the hope that they would come to the race fresher. As the distances of races became less extreme – at one time they had ranged from two or three furlongs to four miles – horses were trained to excel over more standard distances. Some people maintained that they consequently lost something of the toughness and vigour which previously had enabled them to race for four or five seasons. There was, however, little doubt that the temperaments of the majority of horses were vastly improved and one welcome result was the decline in numbers of 'savage' horses which had been a regular feature during the nineteenth century. George Lambton, the man who made training respectable for gentlemen, recalled in this memoirs, *Men and Horses I Have Known*, a frightening encounter with one such animal on the heath at Newmarket:

> I remember on one occasion when I was the only person left on the Limekilns, and it happened this way: it was at the time that I was suffering from my back and could not ride. I was on foot waiting for my horses to come up the gallop when I heard a most extraordinary noise proceeding from the plantation that runs along the side of the Bury road. Then a loose horse dashed out from the trees, and stood there roaring and trumpeting in a way that I have never heard before or since. I at once recognized that it was a noted savage called Prince Simon, owned by the French sportsman, Monsieur Lebaudy, and trained by Golding. My assistant Harry Sharpe was with me, and I hurried him off to turn my string onto the Waterhall ground, out of the way of this mad brute, who would savage anything he came near. Away went Sharpe, and everyone else made themselves scarce . . . I could see and hear Prince Simon charging about

the plantation in a mad state of fury, kicking and biting at the trees. He then went for Golding, who rode a white hack. Golding discreetly left his hack: it was said that he climbed a tree. The pony galloped off towards Moulton, pursued by Prince Simon, and I thought all was well. But somehow the pony eluded his pursuer, and the Prince again appeared on the Limekilns. Standing there, lord of all he surveyed, he was a fine sight, although rather too close to be pleasant. Still, I did not think that he would bother about me on foot, but finding nothing else worth his attention, he suddenly came charging down on me. It was not a pleasant position, as I was more or less of a cripple. I had my shooting stick with me and when he came at me I gave him a crack over the head which made him stand on his hind legs and roar with rage. At this moment, by the greatest piece of luck, Golding's white hack emerged from the trees on his way home. Prince Simon catching sight of him went after him like a dog after a rabbit, and chased him home into his stables, where they managed to let the pony into a box and shut the door on his pursuer. They were not able to catch the savage until late in the afternoon, when, I suppose, being hungry, he went into his box out of his own accord.

Savage horses may have become a rarity, but towards the end of the century a new and more serious menace appeared in the form of doping. It was one of the first major tests of the Jockey Club's ability to assert their authority and successfully combat a blatant malpractice. Doping was introduced from America during the 1890s and immediately began to play havoc with form. It also had a disastrous effect on most of the horses subjected to the usually crudely administered stimulation. One horse won a race only to career uncontrollably into a wall and kill itself.

The greatest number of doped horses were run by two American millionaires, William Gates and James Drake. Both were crooks – Gates probably the worst; his loud-mouthed and aggressive style of gambling brought him the nick-name of 'Betcha-a-million'. The pair installed an American trainer, Enoch Wishard, in their stable. Wishard perfected his doping into an art and his success rate was phenomenal. Time and time again mediocre or bad horses won totally unexpectedly, and the Americans raked in their winnings while the racing establishment looked on, initially uncertain what action they could take. Wishard's horses were ridden by two American brothers, Lester and Johnny Reiff, who were as unscrupulous as their employers. Eventually Lester Reiff was warned off by the Jockey Club in 1901 for a particularly outrageous piece of riding. But it was not until 1904 that the Jockey Club was prepared to declare that doping was contrary to the rules of racing and liable to a penalty of warning off. By this time it was estimated that Gates, Drake and their associates had cleared around £2 million

in bets. While it took the bookmakers a long time to recover, the American gang simply moved over to France where they were able to ply their trade for some years until the French Jockey Club eventually followed the lead of their English counterparts.

The disappearance of dangerous horses was accompanied by the disappearance of the dangerous characters who, for much of the nineteenth century, had terrorized racecourses all over England. During the middle of the century riots were a regular feature, as gangs of crooks who still enjoyed easy access to racecourses set about bookmakers and made off with their day's winnings. By the turn of the century they had been hounded off the Turf by the vigilance of the Jockey Club and the stewards of race meetings; by the increased number of policemen who attended the races; and by the fact that they had become outnumbered by respectable race-goers.

The ordinary Englishman, provided with cheap transport to the races with the advent of the railways, was responsible for the huge increase in race crowds which had occurred by the turn of the century. But it was the adoption of racing by fashionable, upper-class society which invested the sport with a hitherto unknown glamour. Racing had become organized, accessible and respectable; but not too respectable. Beneath the surface there remained a streak of unpredictable excitement which appealed to this fast-living, high-spending set.

Even the police find time for a hearty lunch at the races. Their increasing presence played a large part in ridding the racecourses of a variety of criminals.

Enoch Wishard (right): the American trainer who perfected the art of doping and won a fortune for his crooked employers.

HOUSE PARTIES

Daisy Warwick: very fast.

When Lady Brooke, later the Countess of Warwick and better known as Daisy, was summoned by Queen Victoria to dine and spend the night at Windsor Castle, the royal command interfered with Essex Hunt Races. For Daisy this was an important annual event and she always entertained a large party at Easton Lodge, her Essex home. Early on the morning after the dinner, dressed in a pink riding habit, she left Windsor, defying protocol by both the hour of her departure and the colour of her clothes. She presumed her departure to go unobserved, but it did not escape the eagle eye of the Queen, who stood at an upstairs window muttering, 'How fast. . .how very fast'. Victoria must have shuddered at the thought that at one time she had considered Daisy a suitable bride for her youngest son, Prince Leopold. As it happened, when the Prince met the then eighteen-year-old Frances Maynard, he was already in love with one of his continental cousins. Daisy, for her part, was far more interested in the Prince's better-looking equerry, Lord Brooke, whom she married shortly afterwards.

Queen Victoria may have disapproved, but by the 1870s it was clear that you had to be fast to get on in society – at least, in the circle surrounding the Prince of Wales. Firmly prevented by his mother from taking even the smallest part in affairs of state, or participating in the official role of the

monarchy, the Prince had plenty of time to indulge in an existence which would have appalled his mother and, more particularly, the deceased Prince Consort, but which he relished.

His enthusiasm was more than matched by those who showed themselves only too eager to follow his lead. The aristocratic and fashionable families who saw it as their natural right to be the leaders of Society had had a pretty hard time of it for some years; under Albert's priggish influence, Queen Victoria considered most of them to be disreputable and decadent. Here, at last, was a Prince of Wales who was destined to become Society's new leader, a man after their own hearts.

In marked contrast to his parents, the Prince's limitations on those chosen to join his immediate circle were not restricted to the higher peerage. True, he was never happier than when staying in extreme aristocratic grandeur – at Chatsworth, with the Duke of Devonshire for instance – but he was equally at home when surrounded by the somewhat more *nouveau riche* splendour of one of the Rothschild homes. In 1869 Victoria had flatly refused to bestow a peerage on 'Natty' Rothschild, protesting: 'To make a Jew a Peer is a step the Queen could not consent to.' Some years later she did relent and Natty got his peerage in 1885, by which time he, his brothers and cousins had been entertaining the Queen's son for some time. Their wealth and lavish lifestyle were virtually unparalleled. Describing Mentmore, designed by Sir Joseph Paxton for Baron Meyer Rothschild, Lady Eastlake wrote, 'I do not believe that the Medicis were ever so lodged at the height of their glory.'

Many people were appalled but the Prince of Wales loved it. Luxury and comfort became two important priorities in his life and if the Rothschilds could provide them on a scale no one else could rival he was not going to let the fact that they were Jewish interfere with his fun. When racing at Newmarket he normally stayed in a suite of rooms in the Jockey Club, but he preferred to be entertained by Leopold de Rothschild at Palace House, his suitably named establishment in the town.

Before the emergence of the Prince of Wales and his circle, Society's activities had been largely confined to London. Here the pace was stepped up rapidly; the occasional balls and tedious levees and garden parties being replaced by a far more demanding round of entertainment for which opulence, rather than taste, was the watchword.

During the day teatime was the occasion for private calls, normally because wives could entertain their lovers without fearing that their husbands might barge in at any minute and the men could visit their mistresses without anyone wondering where they had been. Equally important was the daily parade in

Society's meeting place. Hyde Park at the turn of the century.

Hyde Park's Rotten Row, which, by the 1880s, had become a formal ritual. Here one walked, drove or rode and appearance was all important. Daisy Warwick, usually one of the most prominent figures in the parade, described the scene in her memoirs:

> Late afternoon in Hyde Park meant state carriages and barouches, with beautifully dressed occupants, pulled up under the trees. It was not etiquette to handle the reins oneself in the afternoon so we sat on rows of chairs chatting and behaving as if the world we knew, bounded by the Smart Set, was a fixed orbit, as if London – our London – was a place of select social enjoyment for the Circle, as if nothing could change in this best of delightful worlds. Then there would be the clatter of faster horses, and down this mile of drive came the well-known Royal carriage with the beautiful Alexandra, Princess of Wales, bowing right and left as only she could bow, and hats were raised and knees curtsied before seats were resumed and interrupted chatter continued.

At the same time house parties in the country were becoming increasingly popular and important as social events. To a great extent this was encouraged by the easy and comfortable travel provided by the railways. In the past

travelling to one's country seat from London had meant a long journey in a cramped carriage along dirty roads. Now the railway companies, who were delighted to provide for the aristocracy, could whisk you to your destination in a fraction of the time and as often as not deliver you to a private station which many families built conveniently close to their homes. The Prince of Wales had one at Wolverton, near Sandringham, his home in Norfolk. For some people, however, they were not always as private as they might have wished. When the 4th Earl of Lonsdale arrived at Clifton, the family's private station in Westmorland, to begin his reign as lord of nearby Lowther Castle, huge crowds waited to greet him. Unfortunately the young nobleman had so over-indulged on the train that the only view afforded the faithful tenants and estate workers was of him being carried drunk and virtually unconscious on a stretcher to a waiting carriage.

If trains provided the means of getting to a house party, a race meeting provided members of society with their favourite excuse for one. After the Prince of Wales had shown a growing enjoyment of racing as early as the 1860s the sport became, to an extent, *de rigeur*. Few, however, needed any persuasion about the attractions of racing; it provided a way of life to which the Edwardians instantly succumbed, combining leisure with excitement, gambling, an excuse for dressing up and an opportunity for gossip. At the same time, most of them would have agreed with the cavalier Morton Frewen when he remarked, 'It has always seemed to me that in Beauty's domain the beauty of a horse ranks very high.' Horses became animals of almost sacred

Private transport par excellence: The Marquess of Londonderry's personal train, suitably emblazoned on the side with his coronet encircled by the Garter motif. It ran on the private line from the family seat at Wynyard Park, County Durham.

qualities and money was lavished on them in a way that had never been seen before and which was only brought to an end by the arrival of the motor car.

By the turn of the century the scale of some of the house parties attending the race meetings was staggering. For the guests they normally began and ended with a scene similar to that described by Daisy Warwick in her memoirs: 'I remember with amusement the mountains of luggage that were landed at a country station when one of our parties broke up . . . the whole platform from end to end seemed to be piled with luggage, with large coronets and conspicuous letters, and with any number of gentlemen's gentlemen and ladies' maids in attendance.'

For the hostesses the preparations and arrangements resembled a military operation. The sheer manpower needed to keep a large house party running smoothly for up to a week demanded armies of servants who would outnumber the guests by at least two to one. The Duke of Richmond at Goodwood House during the week of racing there at the end of July, or the Duke of Devonshire at Chatsworth and the Duke of Portland at Welbeck during the St Leger week, regularly entertained forty to fifty or more guests in their vast houses. With each guest normally bringing one servant each – and some of the grander ones did not hesitate to bring more – including the resident staff, there could be well over one hundred people in the house.

Frederick Gorst, at one time a footman at Welbeck, left an illuminating picture of the organization of the ducal seat: 'When we served the Duke and Duchess of Portland at dinner there were always three men in attendance; two footmen and either the wine butler or the groom of the chambers. There was no butler on the staff because Mr Spedding was the chief steward or major-domo and unlike smaller establishments this great house required departmental heads and assistants.' He went on to describe the breakdown of the staff around the turn of the century, who totalled between 270 and 300.

Kitchen and Services

Steward
Wine butler
Under butler
Groom of the chambers
4 royal footmen
2 steward's room footmen
Master of the servant's hall
2 page boys
Head chef
Second chef

Head baker
Second baker
Head kitchen maid
2 under kitchen maids
Vegetable maids
3 scullery maids
Head stillroom maid
Hall porter
2 helpers (hall boys)
Kitchen porter
6 odd men

House and Personal Services

Head housekeeper
Duke's valet
Duchess's personal maid
Lady Victoria's personal maid
Head nursery governess
Tutor
French governess
Schoolroom footman
Nursery footman
14 housemaids

Mechanical Help in the Household

6 engineers (house and electric plant)
4 firemen (electric plant and steam heating)
Telephone clerk and assistant
Telegrapher
3 Night watchmen

Stable

Head coachman
Second coachman
10 grooms
20 strappers and helpers

Garage

Head chauffeur
15 chauffeurs
15 footmen
(2 men on the box at all times)
2 washers

Estate Management

Estate manager
(Duke's confidential clerk)
Secretary to the Duke

Chapel

Resident Chaplain
Organist

Titchfield Library

Librarian
Clerk
Housemaids (for dusting)

Racing Stables

Stud groom
15 assistants

Gardens

6 house gardeners (subterranean greenhouses and house decorations)
30–40 gardeners
40–50 roadmen

Home Farm

Head farmer
15–20 men in vegetable gardens and orchards

Gymnasium

Head instructor
Japanese instructor

Golf Course

Head greensman
10 helpers

Laundry Cottage

Head laundress
12 laundresses

Window Cleaners

Head window cleaner
2 assistants.

Usually the guests were quite oblivious to the frenzied activity which kept them comfortable and entertained: the laying and lighting of scores of fires, the fetching of gallons of hot water, the cooking and serving of tons of food – often in kitchens far from the dining-room, along winding corridors or deep

below stairs. Meals were of major importance and racing parties often brought the added complication of having to prepare a lavish picnic to be transported to the racecourse. For these occasions, enormous hampers filled not only with food and drink but also silver, china and glass, were loaded up and transported to the racecourse.

The actual transport could pose considerable problems. If the course was close enough a fleet of carriages – or, later, motor cars – was able to cope with the guests and their requirements for the day. Otherwise it was necessary to go by train, as did Edward VII when he stayed with Lord Savile at Rufford Abbey for the St Leger (which he did for the last eight years of his reign). On these occasions a private train conveyed the party from Rufford station to Doncaster where the carriages were waiting to take them to the racecourse. The servants who were on hand, either to drive the carriages, or serve the

Lunch at the Derby: al fresco *but hardly uncomfortable, with entertainment by the clown.*

picnic or lunch in a private box, were often dressed in livery and there would be nearly as many of them as would later attend the guests at dinner. It was impressive, time-consuming and extremely costly, but one could certainly not afford to leave any eventuality unaccounted for or to make mistakes.

The Prince of Wales was far and away the most important guest and many hosts and hostesses awaited his arrival with as much trepidation as pride. The Prince liked to know who else was staying, expected them to be largely his friends and had the veto on any guest list. If the house was not grand enough, a suite of rooms set aside for his use would possibly have to be redecorated and refurnished for each visit. Meals had to be absolutely punctual and not last too long, for although he liked his food the Prince was easily bored. At the end of a stay the departing royal back was viewed with considerable relief and many a host was left contemplating a bill for a few days which ran into thousands of pounds.

For some the going proved insupportably expensive. Lord Dupplin and Lord Hardwicke both ruined themselves entertaining the Prince, as did poor old Christopher Sykes. An incurable snob, Sykes was quite incapable of saying no to any of the Prince's whims. His home, Brantingham Thorpe, was close to Doncaster and the Prince regularly stayed with him for the St Leger during the 1870s and '80s. For many years Christopher was the butt of the rather basic royal humour. At the same time the expenses he incurred entertaining the Prince were far more than his slim income could bear. By 1890 he was ruined and only just saved from the final humiliation of public bankruptcy when the Prince intervened after a stormy meeting with Christopher's sister-in-law, the notorious Jessica, who upbraided him for causing her brother-in-law's downfall. (As is described later, Jessica's disastrous career made Christopher's problems appear mild in comparison.)

With or without the Prince of Wales the compilation of the guest list for a house party often needed as careful preparation as the domestic arrangements. Despite their obsession with 'form' and the need visibly to maintain standards, most people agreed with Mrs Patrick Campbell's dictum, 'It doesn't matter what you do, as long as you don't do it in the street and frighten the horses.' Affairs between married people, most of whom were friends or acquaintances, were commonplace and accepted so long as they remained discreet. It was soon appreciated that in a life controlled by a formal and often public daily routine a house party was the perfect opportunity to enter into, develop or consummate an affair. Hostesses were expected to know whether a husband and wife wished to be separated, who – if anyone – were their respective mistresses and lovers and whether they should be asked. Couples conducting

Royal guest: the King and other guests at Rufford Abbey for the St Leger.

The Rufford Abbey visitors' book: a catalogue of leading racing and Society figures.

an affair could normally expect to have conveniently positioned bedrooms.

Complications did sometimes occur, as when Lord Rossmore set off one night to visit his lover, to find another gentleman parading outside her door. Rossmore was forced to pass innocently and pretend that he was going for an early morning bath – despite the fact that it was still dark outside. More serious was the supposed occasion when the Prince of Wales came face to face with the Earl of Lonsdale in one of the upstairs passages of Goodwood House, both on their way to visit Lillie Langtry. Despite being the royal mistress during the 1880s 'the Jersey Lily' was well-known for her generosity with her favours. The Prince was not, however, put off and even when he became King the name of Alice Keppel, his mistress for most of the years of his reign, was almost invariably among the guests when he attended a house party.

Despite the potential headaches of a racing party they were normally popular with hostesses, if only because they eliminated the problem of what to do with a houseful of guests between meals. During the morning everyone disappeared to their bedrooms to change out of their breakfast clothes into their dress for the races. They were then away all day and when they returned it was either time to change again for tea or, if too late for that, to attend to the far more serious task of dressing for dinner. At the grandest houses dinner was more like a state banquet, with quantities of jewellery, tiaras, medals and orders sparkling around the enormous table which groaned with food and a display of ornaments. After dinner there was sometimes dancing – Goodwood Week traditionally closed with an enormous ball given by the Duke of Richmond at Goodwood House – but more often cards or other games which usually involved dressing up. Despite the fact that they might have changed their clothes three or four times already during the day, nobody minded ending the day with an appearance in fancy dress to amuse the party.

The ladies could also be relied upon to enjoy a racing party, especially in comparison to one given for shooting – the other compulsive hobby for most Edwardian men. For shooting parties the ladies were confined to the house until lunch, when they were expected to tramp outside and eat either in some makeshift accommodation or, even worse, in the open. During the afternoon the entertainment was to stand with the guns – who did not want to be distracted – and run the risk of catching a cold from the weather, or a headache from the ceaseless volleys of shots. Clothes had to be practical rather than decorative and the only excitement was if your husband – or lover – was shooting better than anyone else.

Racing, by contrast, was very different. For a start most social meetings took place in the summer. More importantly, it was an opportunity to display

The table laid for dinner at Goodwood House: groaning with food and silver.

the most decorative dresses, which had to be different for each day of a meeting. The Edwardians brought fashion to racing and by the turn of the century the picture in the members' enclosure at any of the main meetings was a ceaseless display of extravagant outfits topped by huge hats and parasols. It was competitive, expensive and sometimes caused absolute frenzy. One year Princess Daisy of Pless, an English lady who had married a member of one of the minor German royal families, was summoned at short notice to stay with Edward VII at Windsor Castle for Royal Ascot. Daisy was something of a prude and disapproved of going to tea with Mrs Keppel, where all that the other ladies discussed was their succession of lovers. But whatever she thought of the lifestyle of the King and his friends she fully appreciated the importance of the command to Windsor:

> I could have cried, although of course, I am pleased to have received the invitation – but I wish I had not to accept it! Besides, I have no clothes! I can't go to Vienna now. . .and there is not time either to make them or try them on.

41

The Ladies showing an interest.

A royal party for Ascot, including the King and Queen Alexandra, the Prince and Princess of Wales and the King and Queen of Norway.

I really can't get Ascot dresses in Breslau; and we cannot arrive in London before Sunday the 13th and have to be in Windsor on the 14th.

She did, however, warm to Windsor and appeared to have enjoyed the racing.

We duly arrived at Windsor, and I can imagine few things more delightful than to be invited there for Ascot. One sees the racing in the most comfortable way, meets all one's friends (and enemies), makes – or loses – a little money, and all without any fatigue or bother. . .All my clothes have been a great success and Hans [her husband] said I was the best dressed woman at the races. All very simple and draped; one day a big bunch of pink lilies and my scarab turquoises. Then I twice wore Fritz's gold coat which made a great effect and looked lovely.

To stay at Windsor for Royal Ascot was the height of social acceptability, a privilege reserved for the few. It was also more formal, more proper and far less relaxed than most of the other parties given through the racing season. Some of these became annual events and as the same people were almost invariably present year after year so their feeling of self-assured élitism became more marked. The first of the year was given by Harry Chaplin for the Lincoln meeting, at his nearby home Blankney. Chaplin had begun his racing career as a young man in spectacular style by paying the unheard of sum of £11,000 for two yearlings and soon afterwards he passed into racing legend as the owner of Hermit.

At the time Hermit's victory in the Derby was at the centre of the rivalry between Chaplin and the Marquess of Hastings – an episode which scandalized Victorian society. Hastings was a compulsive gambler and a drunkard who spent most of his time in London visiting disreputable haunts. He once released a sack of rats in a crowded club renowned for its prostitutes and gambling. Most people would not have been seen dead on a racecourse in his company. Chaplin was drawn equally irresistibly to racing and it was said that, 'He bought horses as though he were drunk and backed them as though he were mad.'

In 1864 Chaplin came down from Oxford and during that summer became engaged to Lady Florence Paget, daughter of the Marquess of Anglesey. A renowned beauty, the diminutive lady was known as 'the Pocket Venus'. The wedding never took place because shortly before it was due Chaplin delivered his fiancée to the front door of Marshall & Snellgrove to do some shopping and she disappeared out of the back to elope with Hastings. Not content with stealing Chaplin's bride the wayward Marquess became obsessed with beating his rival on the Turf. In 1867 Chaplin's horse Hermit was a tremendous prospect for the Derby. While Hermit's owner steadily wagered

Harry Chaplin: still hunting when over eighteen stone and a test for any horse.

increasing sums on the horse winning, Hastings bet all he could muster for it to lose. In the event Hermit romped home bringing Chaplin well over £100,000. Hastings lost £120,000 and never recovered. His health was destroyed by drinking and he spent the remaining months of his life trying to recoup his losses with a series of desperate plunges. He died in 1868, aged only twenty-six, a physical wreck and a social outcast who had catastrophically squandered his fortune by gambling. Few people were sorry to see the back of him.

By contrast, Chaplin survived to become a pillar of the establishment as a politician and ended up a Viscount. He also found a wife, Lady Florence Leveson-Gower, a daughter of the Duke of Sutherland, who brought him far more happiness than her fickle namesake would ever have done. Tragically she died only five years after their marriage. Despite his enormous win on Hermit, Chaplin also ruined himself financially. As a young man he had inherited large estates in Lincolnshire from his uncle. By the turn of the century they had all been sold and he was forced to divide his declining years between the many Sutherland seats.

The memory of his patriarchal lifestyle did, however, remain as described by his daughter, Lady Londonderry, in her biography of her father: 'There are still old men who can remember the procession of the Squire of Blankney and his guests to the Lincoln races, the former driving his own four-in-hand,

and the enthusiastic reception which awaited him on the course, only equalled by that accorded to Royalty'. Certainly Chaplin lost none of his zest as a result of his setbacks. Towards the end of his life the fact that he weighed well over eighteen stone did not deter him from frequently appearing in the hunting field, as George Lambton recalls: 'To see him thundering down at a fence on one of his great horses, eyeglass on his eye, was a fine sight. . .The Squire's pluck was marvellous, for it was with the greatest difficulty that he could be got on or off a horse, but once in the saddle he was as happy as a sand-boy'.

Parties for the earlier meetings of the year, such as Chaplin gave for the Lincoln, were something of an exception and it was not normally until the summer that the social activity of the racing world hotted up. Their efforts reached a pinnacle during the week of Royal Ascot by which time every rentable house in the countryside for miles around had been booked for months. Some people – such as the Duke of Westminster who owned Cliveden – were fortunate enough to have their own houses in the vicinity, and these would, without fail, be filled with guests. Although by the turn of the century there were few – if any – events which topped Ascot for importance in the social calendar, it was in some ways more compulsory than enjoyable. Towards the end of her life Daisy Warwick remembered it as a series of, 'stilted, expensive, extensive and over-elaborate garden parties'. It was with considerable relief that many people made their way to Newmarket for the July meeting and on to Goodwood at the end of the month. At both places the atmosphere was far more relaxed. Indeed, Goodwood marked the end of the summer season, and there were many people who retired to houses along the south coast or closer to Goodwood Park as much for a rest as for the racing.

Goodwood: a chance to relax after the summer season.

ROYAL WINNERS

Queen Victoria: unamused by Bertie's racing exploits, but unwilling to allow him a hand in the affairs of state.

In 1867 the Prince of Wales watched Hermit win the Derby from the Royal Box, with Harry Chaplin, who had become a friend during the Prince's somewhat unacademic sojourn at Oxford, by his side. Queen Victoria was less than enchanted with her heir's enthusiasm for the Turf. Shortly before Ascot Week she wrote to him:

> Dearest Bertie,
> Now that Ascot Races are approaching, I wish to repeat *earnestly and seriously*, and with reference to my letters this spring, that I trust you will . . . as my Uncle William IV and Aunt, and we ourselves did, *confine* your *visits* to the Races to the *two* days, *Tuesday* and *Thursday* and not go on *Wednesday* and *Friday*, to which William IV never went, nor did we . . . your example can do *much* for good and do a great deal for evil . . . I hear every true and attached friend of ours expressing *such anxiety* that you should gather round you the really good, steady, and distinguished people.

In an unusually abrupt reply the Prince of Wales made it quite clear that racing was one subject on which he had no intention of being dictated to:

> I fear Mama, that no year goes round without your giving me a jobation on the subject of racing . . . The Tuesday and Thursday at Ascot have always been looked upon as the great days as there is the procession in your carriages up the course, which pleases the public and is looked upon by them as a kind of annual pageant. The other days are, of course, of minor importance, but when you have guests staying in your house they naturally like going on those days also, and it would, I think, look both odd and uncivil if I remained at home, and would excite comment if I suddenly deviated from the course I have hitherto adopted . . . I am always most anxious to meet your wishes, dear Mama, in every respect, and I always regret if we are not quite *d'accord* – but as I am past twenty-eight and have some considerable knowledge of the world and society, you will, I am sure, at least I trust, allow me to use my discretion in matters of this kind.

Victoria continued with her frequent remonstrances on the subject, largely to no avail. The Prince's patronage of racing for the rest of his life was to be the most successful ever enjoyed by a member of the Royal Family. Although they were not surprised by the Prince's desire to become actively involved in racing as an owner, many of his contemporaries were astonished by his remarkable success. Despite having to accept some years of indifferent results, in Persimmon and Diamond Jubilee he bred and owned two of the outstanding horses of the period. In addition to his personal victories his patronage of racing was, without question, the decisive factor in elevating the sport from its somewhat murky past to its lofty position as Society's – and much of the rest of the country's – favourite pastime.

During the 1870s a number of the Prince's friends were already well-established as leading figures of the Turf. Two of them, Sir Frederick Johnstone and Lord Alington, owned horses in partnership with notable success. They were known as 'the Old Firm'. As well as being an expert judge of horseflesh, Johnstone was also a connoisseur of women and in 1870 had been, with the Prince, one of the unfortunate co-respondents in the highly publicized Mordaunt Affair. As a result of the hysterical confessions of the mentally unstable Lady Mordaunt the Prince was forced to make embarrassing history by becoming the first Prince of Wales to appear in the witness-box. The advice of Johnstone and Alington was an important influence on the Prince's decision to embark on a career as an owner. After registering his colours in 1875 the activities of his early years were both modest and unsuccessful. In 1883, in partnership with Lord Alington, he leased two fillies from Lady

John Porter, the most successful trainer of the period. Edward VII was one of the few people to take his horses away from the famous yard at Kingsclere.

Stamford for the season. One of the horses, Geheimniss, had won the Oaks – the major fillies Classic – the year before and it was largely the successes of these two animals which persuaded the Prince to expand his involvement as an owner. It was also through Alington and Johnstone's influence that he made the decisive move of sending his horses to John Porter, who trained for 'the Old Firm' and a number of other leading owners at Kingsclere in Hampshire, where Ian Balding trains today.

John Porter began training at Kingsclere in 1867. By the time he retired in 1905 he had trained the winners of seven Derbys – a record which has never been equalled – as well as sixteen other Classics. It was fortunate that his father, who wanted him to join a lawyer's office and was violently opposed to him going into racing, did not have his way. Quiet, modest and totally dedicated, Porter never gambled and resented anything interfering with his work. On one occasion when he was leaving Brighton races his companion had his watch ripped out of his pocket by a thief. Justifiably indignant, he was all for calling the police. Porter would have nothing of it: 'For heaven's sake be quiet, if you give the thief a charge we may be detained here for weeks and I have other things to do.'

In 1886 the Prince of Wales had his first win in his own colours with a horse called Counterpane, trained by Porter. It seemed, however, that his luck had not turned. In Counterpane's next outing she suddenly collapsed

and died after finishing the race. Porter only trained for the Prince for six years but during that time he laid the foundations of the royal racing successes. In 1885 the Prince had decided to establish his own stud at Sandringham and asked Porter to buy him some mares to breed from. Among the horses Porter bought was Perdita II, for whom he paid £900. At the time Sir Dighton Probyn, who controlled the royal purse, remarked caustically to the trainer when giving him the money for the horse, 'You will ruin the Prince if you go on buying these thoroughbreds.' Many years later the Prince himself was nearer the mark when he told Porter, 'When you bought her you as good as made me a present of a quarter of a million of money.' Perdita II was the dam of all his best horses and her offspring won £73,000 in prize money – the equivalent of £2½ million today.

In 1892 the Prince decided to move his horses from Kingsclere to Newmarket. To an extent his decision was influenced by convenience, for Newmarket was midway between London and Sandringham. It was also at the suggestion of the Prince's racing manager, Lord Marcus Beresford. Lord Marcus was one of three sons of the Marquess of Waterford whose names all loomed large throughout the Edwardian period. The eldest, Lord William,

Perdita II. The Prince of Wales's great brood-mare and foundation of his racing successes.

was a distinguished soldier and won the VC. The youngest, Lord Charles, enjoyed an equally successful career in the navy and ended up as an admiral. All three were renowned sportsmen and Lord Charles's remark after a naval battle on the Nile when he was one of the few survivors, 'It was hard to die without knowing who had won the Derby', was characteristic of their outlook on life. Unfortunately Charlie was as hot-headed as he was hot-blooded and he later fell out disastrously with the Prince over the affections of Daisy Warwick.

Lord Marcus's knowledge of horses was considerable, but he suffered a personality clash with John Porter. The autocratic Lord Marcus expected to have his say in all decisions concerning the Prince's horses while the trainer objected to taking orders from a racing manager. As a result Lord Marcus recommended to the Prince that he move his horses to be trained by Richard Marsh, who had recently moved into palatial new stables at Egerton House in Newmarket – suitable surroundings for the royal horses.

Marsh had become a friend of Lord Marcus as a young man when he enjoyed a successful career as a 'gentleman' rider. After turning to training his main patron, until the arrival of the Prince of Wales, was the Duke of Hamilton. Before taking on the Prince's horses Marsh saw fit to ask the Duke's permission – a decision which caused Lord Marcus considerable embarrassment but which the Prince took as proof of the man's loyalty to his owners.

After two years of training for the Prince, Marsh's opinion of most of the horses which had arrived from Kingsclere was depressingly concise, 'awful'. There was only one exception, a large colt called Florizel II. Florizel II's sire was the Duke of Portland's legendary stallion St Simon and his dam was Perdita II – the breeding combination which brought a touch of magic to the Prince's fortunes. As a three- and four-year-old Florizel II won a number of good races, which included giving the Prince his first successes at Royal Ascot.

In a sense Florizel II was only a forerunner for his full brother, Persimmon, who appeared as a two-year-old in 1895. From his earliest days Persimmon had the look of a class horse and his two victories as a two-year-old were both in prestigious races that in the past had been won by horses which went on to win Classics as three-year-olds. In his third outing he was beaten by St Frusquin, owned by Leopold de Rothschild, the horse that was to be his great rival in the following year.

At the beginning of the 1896 season Persimmon missed the Two Thousand Guineas as a result of an abcess which he had developed in his mouth. The race was duly won by St Frusquin who, on the strength of his victory over

Winning trio: Edward VII with his trainer Richard Marsh (left) and racing manager Lord Marcus Beresford (centre).

Persimmon the previous autumn, had been made firm favourite. Despite the absence of Persimmon the Spring Meeting at Newmarket did not pass without the Prince of Wales achieving a notable landmark in his career when his filly, Thais, carried off the One Thousand Guineas – albeit against mediocre opposition – thereby giving him his first Classic win.

Having recovered his health Persimmon began his preparatory work for the Derby. Unfortunately he started showing the awkward characteristics for

which his mother, Perdita II, had been well known. On one occasion, when Marsh had asked Lord Marcus Beresford to come down to Newmarket and watch Persimmon in a trial, the horse ran so badly that both manager and trainer despaired of his prospects for the great race. Fortunately he pulled himself together and shortly before Derby Day Marsh felt confident enough to suggest to Lord Marcus that he bring the Prince to watch another trial. Marsh had laid out a private gallop at Egerton and here, comfortably seated in a small stand specially erected for the occasion, the Prince, with Princess Alexandra and other members of the Royal Family, was able to watch his horse defeat his rivals in convincing style.

As the Derby approached it seemed that they only had St Frusquin to worry about. On the day, despite the popularity of a royal runner, Leopold de Rothschild's horse was made favourite. As it turned out the bookmakers' forecasts were not to be upheld. In a thrilling contest and one of the closest finishes in the race's history, Persimmon won by a neck. The scene on the course was virtual hysteria as described by one eye witness:

> With what throbbing pulses the Prince had watched this thrilling contest of giants can only be guessed. As for the spectators, the cheers had swelled to a hurricane which must have been heard for miles around. The Prince of Wales had won the Derby! After years of patience and ill-luck at last he had his reward. It was a spectacle such as had never been witnessed before on a racecourse. Members rushed down from the stand to the enclosure, waving their hats as they gazed to where His Royal Highness stood, pale but with a delighted smile on his face . . . winning the Derby always meant much; in the history of the race it had never meant as much as this.

Persimmon went on to win the other major Classic, the St Leger, run at Doncaster in the autumn and later the Jockey Club Stakes at Newmarket. At the end of the season the Prince of Wales's total prize-money amounted to over £26,000 which put him second in the league of winning owners. Between them Thais and Persimmon had won three out of the five Classics.

Although Persimmon's most prestigious wins, the Derby and the St Leger, were achieved as a three-year-old, he reached his peak as a four-year-old. Having won the lucrative Eclipse Stakes he went on to show outstanding versatility by winning the Ascot Gold Cup (run over two and a half miles, as opposed to the mile and a half of the Derby). George Lambton, who had become the Earl of Derby's trainer four years earlier, and whose opinions were universally respected, confirmed Persimmon's quality when he later wrote in his memoirs, 'When Persimmon was stripped for the Ascot Gold Cup he stands out in my memory as the most perfectly trained horse I ever

The Prince of Wales leads in Persimmon after winning the Derby in 1896.

saw, and on that day it would have given my two heroes, St Simon and Ormonde, as much as they could do to beat him.'

Persimmon retired at the end of his four-year-old career by which time he had won nearly £35,000 in stakes, a sum which put him among the most successful horses of the century. Even in the 1890s, with the quantity and value of other top races steadily increasing, the Classics (in particular the Derby and St Leger, and the Oaks for fillies), were still in a league of their own in terms of prestige. Persimmon had brought the Prince of Wales his first victory in the Derby and made him only the second member of the Royal Family in history to attain 'the blue riband of the Turf'. Persimmon was even more of a success financially when he was retired to stud, collecting over £100,000 in stud fees. He was always the Prince's favourite horse and

Persimmon being led out for the Ascot Gold Cup, 1897. 'The most perfectly trained horse I ever saw.' (George Lambton).

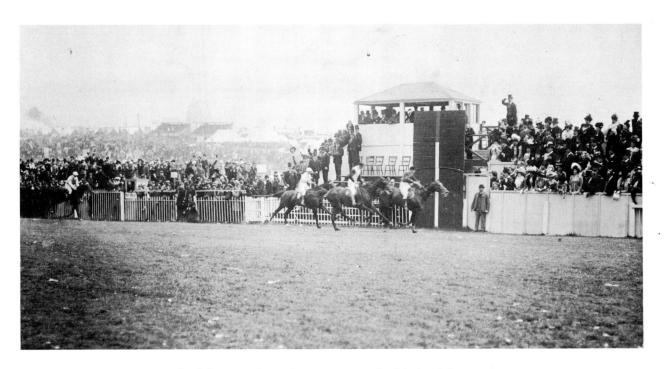

Diamond Jubilee wins the Derby in 1900 – to the delight of the crowd.

when showing his visitors round the stud at Sandringham the royal owner would often stand gazing at the horse, repeating, 'Isn't he beautiful'. When the great horse died of a fractured pelvis in 1908 the Prince ordered Carl Fabergé to model him in solid silver. Perhaps to make up for their Derby defeat and showing a competitive spirit to the last, Mrs de Rothschild immediately ordered the distinguished jeweller to make a similar model of St Frusquin which she presented to her husband Leopold.

Persimmon's victory in the Gold Cup at Ascot in 1897 was the perfect way for the Prince of Wales to celebrate Queen Victoria's Diamond Jubilee. In the same year Perdita II produced another colt by St Simon who was duly named Diamond Jubilee. Although not a horse of Persimmon's overall quality, Diamond Jubilee's three-year-old career in 1900 eclipsed that of his distinguished brother. His prize-money of £28,000 made the Prince of Wales the leading owner for the only time in his career. More important, by winning the Two Thousand Guineas, the Derby and the St Leger he gave the Prince racing's most élite prize, the Triple Crown. Throughout history victory in these three Classics has only been achieved by a handful of horses and owners. Also in 1900, the Prince's horse Ambush II won the Grand National. No one else has ever had the winner of the Triple Crown and the Grand National in one year.

Despite his winning ways Diamond Jubilee was an awkward customer whose temperament was largely to blame for this failure as a four-year-old. As a two-year-old he had sent Sir Dighton Probyn scurrying out of the paddock – not somewhere the dignified courtier frequented more than was necessary. His first jockey was Jack Watts, Marsh's stable jockey, who had ridden Persimmon in all his races. Watts could do little to make Diamond Jubilee behave or even to look like winning a race. After Watts's retirement Mornington 'Morny' Cannon took over and initially enjoyed more success. But when, after one gallop some weeks before the Two Thousand Guineas, Diamond Jubilee seized Morny after he had dismounted and threw him to the ground, Cannon philosophically suggested to Richard Marsh that he find another rider. Marsh's decision to allow Herbert Jones – Diamond Jubilee's stable-lad, for whom the horse had always behaved – to ride him brought the desired effect. Jones rode the horse in all his victories, going on to ride for the Prince of Wales when he became King and later for King George V.

Jones's calming influence notwithstanding, at the beginning of his four-year-old career Diamond Jubilee began to show signs of being not only temperamental but also savage. On one occasion he bit a stable-lad's finger clean off. It was incidents such as this, as well as his disappointing performances

The stud groom's cottage at Sandringham.

in his three races during that year, which led him to be retired to stud at Sandringham at a relatively early age. His success as a sire was never outstanding and he was eventually sold to the Argentine – for the considerable sum of £30,000. It was a disappointing end to the career of a horse that had given the Prince his most successful year – one that most owners only ever dream about.

The Prince of Wales took enormous pleasure in his success as an owner. But equally he enjoyed the background to his victories; watching his horses at exercise, visiting them in their stables at Egerton and preparing the breeding programmes at the stud at Sandringham. If his knowledge and judgement of horses did not match that of his racing manager he always appreciated Lord Marcus's wit, which attended most of his advice. In the early years of his career the Prince was not keen to enter his horses in handicaps. On one occasion when Lord Marcus had persuaded him to enter a horse the Prince thought that the weights were unfair. Rounding on his manager he exclaimed, 'I told you what would happen and I was right,' only to receive the reply, 'Well Sir, if you were King Henry VIII no doubt you could have had the handicapper beheaded, but you can't do that now.'

One of the favourite events in his racing calendar was the traditional Derby Day dinner he gave to the Jockey Club the evening after the race. He had begun giving the dinners during the 1870s and they were held every year, first at Marlborough House and then later at Buckingham Palace when he became King. The winning horse was toasted and its owner – virtually always a member of the Club – responded with a speech. In 1883, when St Blaise won, a slight complication occurred because the horse was owned in partnership by 'the Old Firm'. Almost before the toast was finished Lord Alington was on his feet to make a warm response and steal the show from his less quick-witted partner. Sir Frederick could only rise later and remark

Royal winners. The brass plaques which adorned the boxes of Persimmon and Diamond Jubilee at Sandringham.

caustically, 'May I ask my noble friend where I come in? For I own just as much of the horse as he does; and, though he has omitted to mention my name, he never forgets to send me the bills for training it.' When Persimmon won in 1896 the Prince rounded off a perfect day by leaving his fellow members and going on to supper with Georgina, Countess of Dudley, one of his favourite female companions.

The Prince of Wales never had a large number of horses in training at any time in his career. The total ranged from less than ten in the early years to just over twenty during his reign. Although he won a total of nearly £150,000 in prize-money it was largely thanks to the performances of a handful of horses – Florizel II, Persimmon, Thais, Diamond Jubilee, Minoru and one or two others – and there were many lean years. In these terms he was not among the great magnates of the Turf discussed in Chapter Four. The Dukes of Westminster and Portland, for example, both won more than twice the Prince's figure of total prize-money. Nevertheless, the limited size of his stable compared to some of his aristocratic contemporaries and the years of disappointment emphasize the achievement of his Classic victories.

Perhaps the most unexpected aspect of the Prince of Wales's racing career was the extraordinary degree of popularity which it brought him. When he first appeared at the races after the Mordaunt Affair he was roundly booed by many people in the crowd. Twenty-six years later, when Persimmon won the Derby, the popularity of the Prince, the monarchy and racing reached a spectacular zenith.

No other event in his life produced such a wave of spontaneous affection. One contemporary newspaper wrote, '. . . to a larger circle still he is a typical Englishman, and that is a character which cannot be fully attained except by one who shows himself to be in sympathy with that love of sport which is almost a passion with all ranks and classes in this country.' The German Chancellor, Bismark, certainly agreed when he wrote after one of the royal Derby victories, 'You will never have a revolution in England as long as you keep up your racing.' For most racing crowds the Prince could do no wrong and the knowledge that his bulky but always immaculately dressed figure was on the course changed the atmosphere of any meeting. They loved what Sir Edward Grey described as, his 'rare, if not unique power of combining bonhomie with dignity.' For his part the Prince was always at his best when surrounded by an air of goodwill and he enjoyed some of the happiest and most relaxing moments of his life on the racecourse. His popularity and successes did more to enhance the prestige and social acceptability of racing than any other single factor.

Sandringham. The Prince of Wales's favourite home.

All hats off as the King and Queen arrive at Royal Ascot.

THE RULING FEW

Between 1880 and 1900 three men – the Duke of Westminster, the Duke of Portland and the Earl of Rosebery – bred and owned the winners of twenty-nine Classic races, including eight Derbys, an unprecedented record. They were part of a very small oligarchy who, by virtue of the quantity and quality of their horses and because of their wealth and social power and prestige, dominated the racing world of the Edwardian era. Although, by the turn of the century, racing was no longer the almost exclusive prerogative of the aristocracy that it had been in the past, it was clear that the upper echelons were still controlled by a minority – generations of whose families had enjoyed a similar position in the past. While many owners raced for personal fame and fortune, the great patricians were interested not only in winning but in the general good of racing. They sought improved breeding and training, and better administration. They owned great houses, where they entertained in suitably expansive style during race meetings and their racing establishments were on a scale which has rarely been seen since.

During the 1870s one man, Viscount Falmouth, reigned supreme as an owner. He began racing some years earlier, before he inherited the title, under the assumed name of 'Mr Valentine', possibly to avoid the disapproval of his father who was a clergyman. He inherited his title unexpectedly from a cousin and then considerably increased his wealth by marrying Baroness Despenser whose seat was Mereworth Castle in Kent. Here Lord Falmouth established his stud. Compared to some other mid-century owners, such as Sir Tatton Sykes and Lord Glasgow, both of whom owned hundreds of mainly unnamed and useless horses, Lord Falmouth's stud was not large. But because of his rigorous breeding rules – in particular insisting on only breeding from outstanding mares – the results were spectacular. Between 1772 and 1883 when he retired from racing he never won less than £10,000 in prize money in any year and during his career won a total of around £300,000.

Lord Falmouth's horses were initially trained by John Scott, 'The Wizard of the North', at Malton in Yorkshire. Scott trained the winners of sixteen St Legers (showing the supremacy over their own Classic that Yorkshire trainers achieved until the late nineteenth century), nine Oaks and six Derbys. He

Lord Falmouth, whose horses were unbeatable for a decade in the 1870s and who only ever bet a sixpence.

Fred Archer, whose riding was vital to the successes of Lord Falmouth.

The 1st Duke of Westminster, by Ape.

The stables of the eccentric Sir Tatton Sykes at Sledmeer, Yorkshire. The stable lads surround one of his hundreds of unnamed horses.

supposedly kept touts off the Wolds where he trained by hunting them with a dog from America trained to hunt runaway slaves. When he died in 1871 a contemporary described him as, 'universally regarded as the chief of English trainers, and indisputably first in his profession.'

Lord Falmouth was strongly opposed to any form of gambling and never bet. He only broke his rule once when Mrs Scott, his trainer's wife, bet him sixpence that his filly Queen Bertha would win the Oaks. Lord Falmouth said that the horse did not have a 1,000 to 10 chance and agreed to the bet. The horse won and Lord Falmouth paid up. In characteristic style, he had the sixpence set in diamonds before presenting it to Mrs Scott.

After John Scott's death Lord Falmouth's horses were trained by Matthew Dawson at Newmarket. 'Mat' and his three brothers who were all trainers were born in the unheard-of Scottish town of Gullane where their father was also a trainer. Diminutive and outspoken, with a broad Scots accent which he retained all his life, Mat was a perfectionist and intolerant of owners, jockeys and horses alike. When Lord Falmouth sent his horses to Mat's yard at Heath House, the abrasive Scotsman had secured the most prestigious patron of the day. This did not stop him ordering the removal of the horses, only a few weeks after their arrival. Lord Falmouth had taken the liberty of giving the jockey of one of his horses orders for a race which was subsequently lost. As far as Mat was concerned owners had no business to talk to jockeys and only the intervention of his brother, Joe Dawson, prevented a serious rift.

The other man who played a vital part in Lord Falmouth's successes, along with Mat Dawson, was Fred Archer, for many people the greatest jockey of all time. Archer was apprenticed by Dawson when eleven years old. It was not long before the discerning Scotsman realized that this lanky boy was something special. He was only seventeen when he won the Two Thousand Guineas for Lord Falmouth on Atlantic and for more than ten years the triumvirate was invincible. During the decade of the 1870s they won fourteen Classics.

It has never been clear why, in 1883, Lord Falmouth suddenly decided to give up racing and sell his stud. It was rumoured that he disapproved of the way Archer had ridden his horse Galliard in the 1883 Derby, but it was far more likely that he gave up because of failing health. He died in 1889.

Like Lord Falmouth, the first Duke of Westminster was a man of fastidious character. His only excesses were his fortune and his 344 winners. When he died an obituary in *The Times* said: 'The Duke could pass from the racecourse to a missionary meeting without incurring the censure of even the strictest.' He is the only man in history to have twice bred and owned the winner of

the Triple Crown. He certainly did not need the money being probably the richest man in England. By the turn of the century the income from his London estate alone was in excess of £250,000 per annum, about £8¾ million in today's terms.

In 1875 the Duke laid the foundations of his stud at his home Eaton Hall, Cheshire, when he paid £14,000 for the stallion, Doncaster. It was then, and for many decades afterwards, the highest price ever paid for a single horse. Doncaster had been bred by Sir Tatton Sykes and won the Derby when owned by the uncouth but very wealthy Glasgow ironmaster James Merry. Doncaster may have been expensive but he more than vindicated the Duke's decision. His son Bend Or was the Duke's first Derby winner in 1880, after a sensational race against Robert the Devil. Bend Or was due to be ridden by Archer, but shortly before the race Archer was badly injured in one arm by a horse called Muley Edris. All the same he insisted on riding, despite one arm being virtually useless, and won one of the greatest races of his career. Bend Or's name was perpetuated by the Duke's grandson who succeeded him and was always known as 'Bend Or' after being born in 1879, the year that the horse first appeared as a two-year-old. The Duke did not have to wait long for his next Derby win. In 1882 Shotover achieved the rare distinction of a filly winning the Derby. The year was in fact dominated by a batch of superb fillies who between them won all the Classics. Shotover also won the Two Thousand Guineas and was third in the St Leger in which fillies were uniquely first and second and third.

Over and above his Derby win, Bend Or's greatest contribution was to sire Ormonde. In his memoirs John Porter, who trained the Duke's horses from 1881 onwards, describes the appearance of Ormonde as a two-year-old:

> The year 1885 was a memorable one in the history of Kingsclere, for it was that in which Ormonde made his first appearance on the Turf. I have already expressed the opinion that this horse of Bend Or and Lily Agnes was the greatest horse I have known. There are some of my contemporaries who think St Simon was his superior . . . In any case there is unanimity on one point – both were wonderful animals.

Ormonde's racing career was certainly unparalleled. He was never beaten in sixteen races including the Triple Crown which he was only the fourth horse in history to win. Most significant, in almost all his races he was competing against other top-class horses, for the years of the mid-1880s were the richest of the century for great horses. After a triumphant three-year career it seemed a disastrous blow when during the winter of 1886–87 Porter discovered that

Ormonde was a 'roarer'. Roaring was a fairly common affliction during the nineteenth century: probably the main scourge of race horses as it caused severe breathing problems and normally ruined their racing career. Porter described how on one occasion when they were working Ormonde on the downs in thick fog he could be heard breathing half a mile away. Despite his affliction Ormonde won three times as a four-year-old including probably his greatest victory in the Hardwicke Stakes at Royal Ascot, when he beat Minting – his outstanding rival the year before – and Bendigo.

George Lambton wrote of the Duke of Westminster, 'I question if there was ever a man with greater knowledge of breeding, racing and the training and riding of horses.' Only on one occasion did he allow his curiosity to get the better of his judgement. He was watching Ormonde exercise with Porter and told the trainer that he wished to ride Ormonde. Porter, knowing the horse's enormous strength immediately said it was not a good idea, to which the Duke replied curtly, 'Are you the owner of the horse Mr Porter or am I?' But once mounted the Duke realized that he was almost powerless to stop the animal and was carried considerably further and faster than he would have liked. Afterwards he said, 'Although I have ridden all my life it was the most disagreeable experience I ever went through . . . I knew perfectly well that I had absolutely no control over the beast at all.'

In June 1887 the Duke held a huge garden party at Grosvenor House in London in honour of Queen Victoria's Jubilee and Ormonde was the guest of honour. Porter brought him up from Kingsclere by train to Waterloo and then walked him across London to Park Lane. During the party Ormonde stood on the lawn being admired by all the guests and fed by some of them, including the Queen of Belgium, who gave him handfuls of carnations.

A few years after Ormonde had retired to stud the Duke was widely criticized for selling him to the Argentine. His decision was, however, based on the sound belief that roaring was hereditary and would be carried to Ormonde's offspring. The horse did, nevertheless, spend two seasons at stud at Eaton when he sired Orme, his outstanding offspring. Orme's career was largely spoilt by ill fortune. Just before he was due to run in the Two Thousand Guineas he suddenly became sick. It was suspected that he had been poisoned with mercury – to the extent that the Duke published a notice offering £1,000 reward for information leading to the conviction of the guilty party. He missed both the Two Thousand Guineas and Derby, then after making a miraculous recovery lost in the St Leger largely through the stupidity of his jockey, Barrett, who wore the horse out by jumping off in front.

Orme did win a number of good races, including the Eclipse Stakes twice

*Bend Or. The Duke of Westminster's first Derby winner, and sire of the
legendary Ormonde.*

which largely accounted for his winnings of £32,000. More important was
his success at stud. In 1896 he sired the Duke's second Triple Crown winner
Flying Fox. Flying Fox's mother was a foul-tempered mare, suitably named
Vampire, which Porter had bought for the Duke three years earlier. When
she first arrived at the Eaton Stud she mauled a groom and even had the
effrontery to attack His Grace himself when he went to visit her. She then
killed her first foal in a fit of rage. Flying Fox inherited her temperament and
his appearance in the Two Thousand Guineas caused the normally reticent
Duke to lose his self-control for the only time in his life. Flying Fox was hot
favourite but refused to behave at the start, continually bolting off into the
country despite the efforts of his luckless jockey 'Morny' Cannon. When it
seemed almost certain that the race would start without him the Duke left
the Jockey Club stand, from where he had been anxiously watching his horse's
antics, and sat down by George Lambton saying, 'This is one of the most

painful moments of my life.' Against all odds however they did manage to get the race started with Flying Fox among the runners. As he passed the post the winner, the Duke was on his feet with excitement and, as Lambton described, 'let out a piercing "View Holloa" which re-echoed through the Stands. The shocked amazement of the Duke's friends was comical to see. No member of the Jockey Club had ever committed such an atrocity . . .'

Flying Fox's career, climaxing in 1899, when he won the Triple Crown, was a fitting end to the Duke's racing successes and he died shortly before the end of that year. His horses were sold the next year, many achieving record prices. Flying Fox was sold to a Frenchman for 37,500 guineas but proved a cheap investment as he sired the winners of over £200,000. For nearly three decades the Duke enjoyed almost unbroken success. Despite his reserve he was enormously popular, on and off the course. One loyal vicar in Chester was regularly known to pray in church for his patron's horses before they ran in an important race. Neither was the Duke without humour. One day at Eaton he was accosted by an unsuspecting visitor who enquired who lived in the enormous mansion and in the same breath asked to be shown round. Without revealing his identity His Grace politely obliged and at the end of the tour was rewarded with half a crown. Among race-goers it was reckoned that you could, 'back a Westminster horse and be sure of a run for your money.' Even for a man of his means his generosity to charitable causes was never ending. When Flying Fox won the Eclipse Stakes in 1899 the Duke

Eaton Hall, the Duke of Westminster's massive pile in Cheshire.

gave the winning stake of £10,000 to the Royal Alexandra Hospital at Rhyl. The importance of his stud at Eaton largely came to light in future years in the offspring of successive generations and as well as the quantity of outstanding horses he bred and owned he had the satisfaction of having produced, in Ormonde, one of the greatest race horses in history.

The man who owned the other horse with a claim to be the 'race horse of the century' was, suitably enough, another Duke. If the Duke of Westminster's fortune derived largely from his relatively small but priceless quantity of acres in London, the 6th Duke of Portland's came from the 183,000 acres he owned in England and Scotland – in particular from the coal beneath large tracts of his Nottinghamshire estates. The grand total put him near the top of the mighty league of twenty-eight men who, in 1883, owned over 100,000 acres. His family had been leading figures in racing for many generations, most notable among them Lord George Bentinck. During the 1830s and 1840s Lord George, younger son of the 4th Duke of Portland, had been the dominant figure on the Turf and established a personal authority which made him, with Charles Bunbury before and Admiral Rous afterwards, one of the three Dictators of the Turf. A heavy better himself, he nonetheless launched a series of open attacks on the criminal aspects of racing, sometimes with considerable results. He enjoyed regular success as an owner but victory in the Derby, which became a consuming ambition, always eluded him. In the end he was cheated by Fate. The year after he had retired from racing – to become more active as a politician — a horse bred by Lord George won the Derby for its new owner.

The Duke first became involved in racing in 1880 and although he began to lose interest towards the end of his life it was certainly not through lack of success. During the early years of his career his horses were trained by Mat Dawson, who appreciated the Duke's timely arrival on the racing scene, as he was to become Dawson's main patron after the retirement of Lord Falmouth.

It was Dawson who was partly responsible for the greatest coup of the Duke's career, the purchase of St Simon. St Simon had been bred and owned by Prince Batthyany, a Hungarian whose one passion in life was racing in England. His horses were trained by Mat Dawson's brother John, who constantly feared for the Prince because he got so excited when his horses were running. His fears proved well founded. In 1883, while watching Galliard – which was sired by his horse, Galopin – in the Two Thousand

Welbeck Abbey, the Portland seat in Nottinghamshire.

Guineas, the Prince got so over-excited that he had a heart attack and dropped dead. As a result his horses were sold later in the year.

St Simon's sire, Galopin, had opened the Edwardian era by winning the Derby in 1875. Galopin went on to be a prodigious sire and was leading sire in 1898 when aged twenty-six. Despite the claims of Ormonde, St Simon was with little doubt the most important horse of the period. When the sale of Prince Batthyany's horses came up St Simon was a two-year-old at John Dawson's stable. The Duke of Portland attended the sale with Mat Dawson who pointed out St Simon to him. When they looked at the horse he had a white dressing on one hock but, unlike many people who thought it was a dressing for some injury, Mat Dawson supposedly just muttered something about his crafty brother John and walked away. At the sale the Duke instructed Mat Dawson to go on bidding for St Simon until he told him to stop and they were successful at 1,600 guineas, according to George Lambton, 'assuredly the cheapest horse that was ever sold.'

Although St Simon did not run in any of the Classics, due to the death of Prince Baltyhany he was unable to enter, he was never beaten – in fact never extended. As a four-year-old he won the Ascot Gold Cup by twenty lengths at a canter. It was reported that the jockey could not pull him up until nearly

a mile past the post. Mat Dawson said that he had never seen a horse so full of 'electricity' – which probably accounts for his unsettled temperament. It is not surprising that his stable lad was once heard to mutter, 'It's all very well to talk about the patience of Job, but Job never had to groom St Simon.' On one occasion St Simon chased the poor chap under the manger in his box and was in the act of dragging him out with his teeth when help arrived.

St Simon ended his racing career as a four-year-old. As George Lambton remarked, 'He had educated the public as to what a high-class thoroughbred should be.' Mat Dawson's opinion was characteristically succinct. 'I have only trained one smashing good horse in my life – St Simon.' His one comment on the never-ending St Simon–Ormonde rivalry was, 'Well, John Porter says that Ormonde was the best horse he ever trained. I say that St Simon was the best horse I ever trained, and I am damned sure that I trained as good horses as John Porter.'

Electrifying though he was as a racehorse, it was St Simon's success as a sire which established his importance in racing history. His record was staggering. His offspring won over £550,000. Ten colts and fillies between them won seventeen Classics. St Simon was nine times leading sire, including consecutively between 1890, when his first three-year-olds ran, and 1896. In 1900 his offspring won all the Classics.

Second in importance to St Simon in laying the foundations of the Duke of Portland's racing successes was Mowerina, a mare which the Duke purchased from Lord Rossmore in 1881 for £1,400 – the sum the erratic Irish peer needed to pay off his debts from a recent meeting. After Mowerina had been at the Duke's stud (at his home, Welbeck Abbey) for some years the

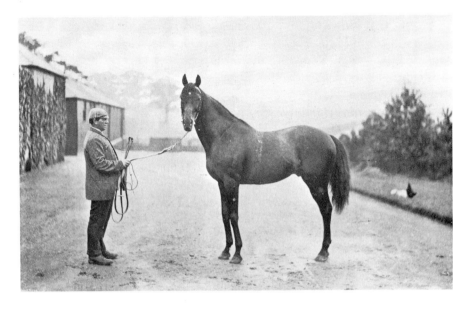

St Simon. Unbeaten as a racehorse and sire extraordinaire.

*The 6th Duke of Portland, in his uniform as
Master of the Horse.*

Duke was going round with his agent who remarked, looking at Mowerina, 'That mare has been worth her weight in gold.' Disbelievingly the Duke told him to prove it and the result was that the horse weighed nine and a half hundredweight and her offspring had won the equivalent of thirteen hundredweight of gold sovereigns.

The best horse that Mowerina produced was Donovan, the Duke's second consecutive Derby winner in 1889; his horse Ayrshire having won in 1888. Like St Simon, Donovan was sired by Galopin, and, despite only running as a two- and three-year-old, was the Duke's most prolific success, winning eighteen out of twenty-one starts and a total of £55,154. This record was broken in the 1890s by Isinglass, but as the Duke quite justifiably pointed out, Donovan's wins were only during two seasons while Isinglass's were spread over three.

In the year that Donovan won the Derby the Duke of Portland was serving as Queen Victoria's Master of the Horse. On one official engagement in this capacity he experienced an embarrassing if satisfying incident. He was accompanying the German Kaiser through the City of London when someone called out from close by in the crowd, 'Damn the Kaiser! Three cheers for

good old Donovan!' Even worse was an occasion when, as Master of the Horse to King Edward VII, the Duke was responsible for the royal transport from Windsor Castle to Ascot races. It was not one of the royal parade days so the King had chosen a rather elderly and unused carriage to ride in. Lord Burnham, who was driving, had both new reins and gloves. The upshot was that the horses bolted going down the Long Walk from the Castle and Burnham was unable to hold them while the carriage careered along for some distance with its passengers – the King, the Earl of Pembroke, the Portuguese Ambassador (the Marquess de Soveral) and the unfortunate Portland – rattling around inside like peas in a pod. Eventually the horses were brought under control, but, when they arrived at the races, Portland continued to experience a day when he could do nothing right. He added insult to injury when his horse beat the King's in one of the races.

The Duke of Portland lived to the age of eighty-five, but enjoyed his best years on the Turf as a young man in his twenties and thirties. Like the Duke of Westminster at Eaton it is likely that he got as much enjoyment out of his stud at Welbeck as he did out of owning winners. The stabling at Welbeck was on a similar scale to the house, which one visitor described as 'vast, splendid and utterly comfortless'. In addition there was an indoor riding school – the second largest in Europe – built by the 5th Duke, an eccentric recluse.

The 5th Earl of Rosebery was another man who began his racing career at a precociously young age. When aged twenty-two he was sent down from Oxford for owning horses. Quite unabashed he wrote to his mother shortly afterwards, 'Dear mother, I have left Oxford. I have secured a house in Berkeley Square; and I have bought a horse to win the Derby. Yr affectionate Archie.' In the event the horse, Ladas, came last in the Derby, but twenty-five years later another of the same name brought Rosebery the first of his two consecutive wins in the race.

Rosebery was always supposed to have had three ambitions in life; to marry an heiress, to be Prime Minister and to own a Derby winner. He achieved all three. In 1878 he married Hannah Rothschild, the only daughter of Baron Meyer Rothschild, whose father had bequeathed her both a fortune of millions and Mentmore, his palatial home. In 1894 Rosebery became Prime Minister and a few months later Ladas II won the Derby. The next year, shortly before Rosebery resigned from office, Sir Visto repeated the victory and in 1905 Rosebery won the race for the third time with Cicero.

Partly because of circumstances beyond his control, but also as a result of

his complex character, Rosebery's premiership, which only lasted fifteen months, was a miserable period of his life. He made his misgivings about becoming Prime Minister clear to Edward Hamilton when they dined together shortly before he took office. 'I call you to witness that I undertake the duty of forming an administration with the utmost reluctance.' His mood had not changed by the time he left office and he wrote in his diary after his final audience with Queen Victoria; 'To London – free.' He was later to write, 'There are two supreme pleasures in life, one is ideal the other real. The ideal is when a man receives the seals of office from his Sovereign. The real pleasure comes when he hands them back.'

In the face of his political problems the victories of his two Derby winners were among his rare bright spots. Yet one of the things that pained him most was the reaction of many of his Liberal colleagues. The 'Nonconformist Conscience' thought it immoral and disgraceful. Later he wrote somewhat bitterly:

> I made the discovery which came to me late in life, that what was venial and innocent in a Secretary of State or a President of the Council was criminal in the First Lord of the Treasury. I do not even know if I ought not to have learned another lesson – that although without guilt or offence, I might perpetually run seconds and thirds, or even run last, it became a matter of torture to so many consciences if I won.

Rosebery was undoubtedly one of the most enigmatic figures on the Turf, respected by most of his contemporaries but known intimately by few of them. His attitude to racing and his involvement in the sport reveal the same contradictions which were evident throughout his political career. Second only to his books, racing was the passion of his life, and yet when speaking to the Gimcrack Club in 1897 he said:

> If I am asked to give advice to those who are inclined to spend their time and their money on the Turf I should give them the advice that *Punch* gave to those about to marry – don't . . . I will give my reasons for that remark. In the first place, the apprenticeship is exceedingly expensive; in the next place, the pursuit is too engrossing for anyone who has anything else to do in this life; and, in the third place, the rewards, as compared with the disappointments, stand in the relation of, at the most, one per cent.

Unlike most of the other great owners of his time he was a lamentable horseman and a singularly bad judge of horses. And yet his wins put him easily among the most successful. There is no doubt that part of his success derived from the enormous sums of money he spent on his stud at Mentmore,

The 5th Earl of Rosebery. The first and only Prime Minister to own a Derby winner.

The Duke of Devonshire, looking respectable for political duties.

Chatsworth at the turn of the century: bastion of ducal splendour.

but beneath his apparent disinterest there was genuine enthusiasm for both racing and the peripheral life that went with it. Writing to his son-in-law, Lord Crewe, he said, 'The noise, stench and villainy of the town of Doncaster are essentially part of the entertainment.'

The scale of Rosebery's stud, where he bred well over five hundred horses during his career, reflected the overall level of his lifestyle which often surprised those who believed him and his wife to be notably unostentatious. Entertainment at Mentmore was sumptuous, and relied on scores of servants who seemed to have no problem filling one of the largest piles in England. Invitations were normally limited to a select circle including many of Hannah's myriad Rothschild relations. On one occasion when the family were predominant at a dinner party, Rosebery decided it was time for bed by calling, 'To your tents O Israel!' When in England rather than at his Scottish homes he spent most of his time at The Durdans near Epsom, which he had bought in 1872 to be close to the racecourse.

When Ladas won the Derby it was typical of Rosebery that he was more upset by the reaction of a Liberal minority than gratified by the wave of national affection which greeted the first victory in the race by a Prime Minister. Sensitivity to criticism dogged him all his life and in 1870 caused him to retire from racing after only a year of ownership, when a critical letter appeared in a sporting newspaper. His return was well received for he brought to the sport the prestige of a leading political figure. The benefit of his undeniably brilliant mind was appreciated by the Jockey Club at a very early stage. They elected him a member at the age of twenty-two. With acute powers of observation he filled his meticulous betting books with snippets of information, as often about political affairs as the fortunes of his horses. If his occasional absences from the political arena to attend a race meeting or watch his horses at exercise were deplored by a number of his colleagues, Rosebery's involvement in the sport was applauded by racing society and the general public in a manner which echoed the welcome of the Prince of Wales.

Another leading political figure who shared Rosebery's affection for racing was the Marquess of Hartington, later the 8th Duke of Devonshire. Despite his Liberal sympathies, Hartington did not always share Rosebery's political views. When he cheered Rosebery's speech, replying to the King's proposal of Cicero's health at the former's Derby dinner in 1905, Rosebery wrote in his diary: 'This was greeted with a loud hoarse cheer – from Hartington – the only cheer I tell him he ever gave me!'

Lord Hartington had no need to marry an heiress to become one of the wealthiest men in England. Like the Duke of Portland he was one of the 100,000-acre men, owning 200,000 acres which brought him rents of £180,000 a year. His family, the Cavendishs, were terribly grand and had been since Tudor times. There was an occasion when the estate steward to a previous Duke was forced to complain to his master about the spendthrift ways of the Marquess of Hartington of the time. 'My Lord Duke, I am very sorry to have to inform your Grace that Lord Hartington appears disposed to spend a great deal of money.' The ducal reply was: 'So much the better Mr Heaton . . . so much the better. Lord Hartington will have a great deal of money to spend.'

Lord Hartington, or 'Harty-Tarty' as he was universally known, was unambitious, diffident, sleepy and forgetful. He once remarked, 'I think my motto should be: never do today what you can put off until tomorrow, and then very often it need not be done.' There were very few things in his life that he was passionate about: one of them was racing. Even so he had the same attitude towards success on the Turf as to most things: 'Sometimes I dream that I am leading in the winner of the Derby, but I am afraid that it will never be anything but a dream.' The closest he got was in 1898 when his horse Dieudonné started second favourite. On that occasion even the impassive Duke was unable to light his habitual cigarette until after the race as his hand was apparently shaking so much, but by then it was too late as Dieudonné had been beaten. In 1877 Belphoebe won the One Thousand Guineas, his only Classic win in over forty years.

Lord Hartington did not indulge in racing to win but for enjoyment, which often eluded him as he was so easily bored. 'I have six houses, and the only one I really enjoy is the house at Newmarket.' In fact he had rather more than six but was apt to forget one or two of them. When an acquaintance was enthusing about Pevensey Castle, which Hartington owned, he got the reply, 'Pevensey . . . whose is Pevensey?'. His two best horses were Morion, who won the Royal Hunt Cup and the Ascot Gold Cup, and Marvel who won the Steward's Cup twice. Unfortunately neither of them were much success at stud, but Hartington was always philosophical abut failure. Towards the end of his life he owned a horse which won at Kempton and was entered for a subsequent race at Newmarket, but had to be withdrawn after being injured in transit. The owner's resigned comment to his trainer was, 'Well, Darling, we had a good time at Kempton.'

Lord Hartington succeeded to the dukedom in 1891 at the age of fifty-nine. By then he had long been one of the Prince of Wales's closest friends

and it became an annual tradition for the Prince to spend the New Year at Chatsworth. On these and other occasions the Duke appeared oblivious to the splendour of the entertainment going on in 'the Palace of the Peak' and was happiest when discussing racing with the Prince. During the period of court mourning after the death of Queen Victoria, King Edward VII leased his horses to the Duke. Only he could have got away with breaches of etiquette such as appearing in front of the Prince wearing his Garter star upside-down. Queen Victoria was not so indulgent on another occasion when, instead of kissing the proffered royal hand, the Duke absent-mindedly shook it. He once forgot that he had Edward VII coming to dinner in London and had to be speedily extracted from the Turf Club.

A royal house party for Doncaster races at Chatsworth, always one of Edward VII's favourite houses. He is standing in the centre, wearing the curly-brimmed bowler which he made fashionable. His host, the Duke of Devonshire, is seated on the left.

One of the Duke's employees at Chatsworth was certain that his master would have preferred to win the Derby with a horse he had bred himself than be Prime Minister. Throughout his long and distinguished political career he displayed rare probity and common sense but no ambition for office. In contrast to a colleague in the House of Commons, who pompously announced that making his maiden speech was the proudest moment in his life, the Duke's proudest was when, as a child, his pig won first prize at Skipton fair. As often as not dispatch boxes which he had looked at were returned with the occasional inadvertent note to his trainer or betting ticket. Throughout his many years as a Cabinet Minister the days of major race meetings were invariably avoided when planning Cabinet meetings. One of his Prime Ministers referred to them as, 'Devonshire's Holy Days'.

In 1907 the Duke of Devonshire had a heart attack while staying with Edward VII at Windsor Castle for Royal Ascot. He never recovered fully and died early the following year in Cannes. His last words were, 'Well, the game is over and I am not sorry.' Of all the great aristocratic owners he was the least successful, but more than any other he enriched the racing world with his unique, eccentric individuality. His distinguished, if untidy figure became one of the best-known and best-loved on the racecourse, while the scale of hospitality at Chatsworth, Devonshire House in London and his other various homes was the envy of most of his contemporaries.

The Duke of Devonshire studies the form.

TABLE OF CLASSIC WINNERS OWNED BY
VISCOUNT FALMOUTH, THE DUKE OF WESTMINSTER, THE DUKE OF PORTLAND AND THE EARL OF ROSEBERY.

	2,000 GUINEAS	1,000 GUINEAS	DERBY	OAKS	ST LEGER
FALMOUTH (Total:18½)	Atlantic (1874) Charibert (1879) Galliard (1883)	Hurricane (1862) Cecilia (1873) Spinaway (1875) Wheel of Fortune (1879) †Busybody (1884)	Kingcraft (1870) Silvio (1877) †Harvester (1884)	Queen Bertha (1863) Spinaway (1875) Jannette (1878) Wheel of Fortune (1879) †Busybody (1884)	Silvio (1877) Jannette (1878) Dutch Oven (1882)
WESTMINSTER (Total:11)	Shotover (1882) ★Ormonde (1886) ★Flying Fox (1899)	Farewell (1885)	Bend Or (1880) Shotover (1882) ★Ormonde (1886) †Flying Fox (1899)		★Ormonde (1886) ★Flying Fox (1899) †Troutbeck (1906)
PORTLAND (Total:11)	Ayrshire (1888)	Semolina (1890) Amiable (1894)	Ayrshire (1888) Donovan (1889)	Memoir (1890) Mrs Butterwick (1893) Amiable (1894) La Roche (1900)	Donovan (1889) Memoir (1890)
ROSEBERY (Total:11)	Ladas (1894) Neil Gow (1910) Ellangowan (1923)	Chelandry (1897) Vaucluse (1915) Plack (1924)	Ladas (1894) Sir Visto (1895) Cicero (1905)	Bonnie Jean (1883)	Sir Visto (1895)

Horses marked with a † were bred by the owner shown but raced by another.
Horses marked with a ★ won the Triple Crown.
Lord Falmouth won 18½ because Busybody dead-heated in the Derby with Harvester.

DISASTER AND SCANDAL

Sir George Chetwynd.

Not everybody could afford to finance their racing careers with the untroubled ease of the great Turf magnates. A number of owners were almost constantly in debt and often teetered on the verge of bankruptcy. For many of them heavy betting offered a means to maintain their position and the all-important outward signs of success. Sir George Chetwynd was for many years a successful owner. He was also a member of the Jockey Club and at one time held the position of Senior Steward – the Club's highest office. It was, however, widely known that his personal finances were not sufficient for his expensive lifestyle and that he largely covered his racing costs by betting. He was, effectively, a professional punter. In 1887 Sir George was the main protagonist in a scandal which shook the racing world and brought his career to a ruinous end.

Sir George's horses were trained at Newmarket by 'Buck' Sherrard. His jockey was Charlie Wood. Wood was as money-minded as Sir George and with such an ostensibly respectable figure behind him breached the rules of racing with impunity. Jockeys were not allowed to own horses but many of the animals owned on paper by Sir George were, in fact, Wood's property. In return, Sir George was able to ensure that his betting paid by gaining the collaboration of his jockey.

Chetwynd House, where Sherrard trained, was owned by Wood. The stable had acquired a reputation for being popular with a number of owners who, like Sir George, were heavy gamblers. By 1887 the rumours had become open scandal; in particular there was speculation that Wood was 'pulling' horses to ensure that Sir George's bets paid off. The first blow fell for the jockey. *The Licensed Victuallers Gazette* published an article, part of which ran, 'How about the running of Success at Lewes and at Alexandra Park, where Charlie Wood nearly pulled his head off on each occasion.' It was an open accusation and Wood sued for libel. Unfortunately when the case came up the jury did not share his outrage. Rather, they showed their opinion of his behaviour by awarding him the derisory sum of one farthing damages.

The next stage was far more serious. At the annual Gimcrack Club Dinner in York in December 1887, the Earl of Durham made a speech which contained scarcely veiled references to the way in which a certain stable in Newmarket conducted its business. In short, he said, the stable and some people involved with it were a disgrace to racing. The accusation could not have come from a more powerful quarter. After the death of Admiral Rous Lord Durham had taken on his role as the leading figure in the administration of racing. Lord Durham made his position even clearer when he wrote to one of the other owners with horses at Chetwynd House saying that he had no intention of implicating him or any other of the stable's patrons; with the exception of Sir George Chetwynd.

Faced with the accusation of indulging in racing fraud Sir George's first reaction was to challenge Lord Durham to a duel. As that was impossible in the 1880s he sued the Earl for libel, claiming £20,000 damages. When the case came into court the outcome was by no means certain and Sir George had a number of powerful supporters including the Duke of Beaufort, General Owen Williams and, it was rumoured, the Prince of Wales himself. His racing manager, Lord Marcus Beresford was one of Lord Durham's few outspoken supporters, for although many people agreed with him in principle most of them were violently opposed to the public exposure of a court case.

In court Lord Durham was represented by Sir Charles (later Lord) Russell, a leading barrister and a noted expert on racing. He was assisted by George Lewis, who was later knighted, the most famous solicitor of the day. George Lewis was almost inevitably involved with any case concerning leading members of society. He was

George Lewis: Society's solicitor and as adroit at keeping people out of the courts as he was at defending them in court. By Spy.

The Earl of Durham.

particularly sought after because of his ability to keep things out of court. In the *Dictionary of National Biography* he is described with some degree of exaggeration as a solicitor who 'gradually obtained what was, for more than a quarter of a century, the practical monopoly of those cases where the seamy side of society is unveiled, and where the sins and follies of the wealthy classes threaten exposure and disaster.' Many members of society heaved large sighs of relief when they heard he had burnt his files after his retirement.

As the case developed Sir George Chetwynd remained both cool and totally confident in his answers to questions. But eventually relentless cross–examination by Sir Charles Russell began to reveal the questionable nature of the financial deals between Sir George and Wood; certainly not the normal arrangement between an owner and his jockey. To the last Sir George maintained both his own innocent position and his jockey's. He was widely admired for his courage and for the manner in which he refused to try and shift any blame to Wood – which he could easily have done to clear himself. The assessors of the case were, however, unconvinced by his arguments. Although they conceded that Sir George had been libelled by Lord Durham, another award of one farthing damages showed their true opinion on the

matter. Sir George's only comment on the verdict, which he heard while racing at Alexandra Park was: 'Rather short odds'. Despite his cool reaction it meant disaster for Sir George: his obligatory resignation from the Jockey Club and the end of his career as an owner. Wood was warned off for a number of years. After some time though, the Jockey Club decided that he had served his punishment and he was allowed to return as a jockey. To show that any acrimony from the case had been buried, Lord Durham offered him his first ride and Wood soon showed that he had lost none of his skill, going on to win the Triple Crown on Galtee More in 1897.

Although never widely liked because of his reserve and aloofness, Sir

The Tranby Croft house party. Standing, left to right: General Owen Williams, Lord Coventry, Lycett Green, Berkeley Levitt, Mrs Lycett Green, Arthur Somerset, Reuben Sassoon, Lord Edward Somerset, Arthur Wilson (son), Tyrwhitt Wilson, Arthur Wilson (father), Christopher Sykes, Count Ludskew. Seated: Miss Naylor, Mrs Owen Williams, Mrs Arthur Wilson, Sir William Gordon Cumming, the Prince of Wales, Countess Coventry, Lady Brougham.

George greatly enhanced his prestige with a number of people as a result of the ordeal to which he had been subjected during the trial. As one contemporary account ran:

> I wonder how many men in the City of London would have passed through such an ordeal as Sir George Chetwynd has done with so much credit. I do not think there are many who would care to have every action of their career, and every document connected therewith, brought into the fierce light that beats upon the witness-box during a cross-examination by Sir Charles Russell.

Most people would have preferred the case to remain out of court and some of them felt that Lord Durham should have followed Sir George's lead and resigned his membership of the Jockey Club as the case had shown him to be guilty of libel. One day at Sandown some time after the case Lord Durham saw Sir George standing in the Jockey Club stand and asked Sir Frederick Johnstone what right he had to be there. 'If you mean you want me to turn George Chetwynd out of this stand I'll see you damned first!' was the forthright reply. Despite never being actively involved again, Sir George retained his interest in and profound knowledge of racing and eventually, at the suggestion of Leopold de Rothschild, a reconciliation was brought about between him and Lord Durham.

The Chetwynd v Durham libel case cast a shadow over the racing world, but it did not compare for sensation and repercussions with the most publicized scandal of the period, the Tranby Croft Affair, or the Baccarat Case, which blew up in 1890. The circumstances of the affair – a gentleman cheating at cards during a house party for the St Leger at Doncaster, would have been public dynamite enough. Worse still, the Prince of Wales was a guest at the house party. The Prince of Wales, his friends and the Turf were subjected to an onslaught of virulent attacks – not only from Englishmen but from Europe and America. It seemed to many people that the façade of wealth, social prestige and gentlemanly conduct had been stripped away to reveal cheating, dishonesty, excessive gambling and a thoroughly despicable and immoral lifestyle. Never had the opponents and critics of the monarchy, the Prince and the upper classes had such an opportunity for attack. They took to their task with relish and at times devastating effect.

In previous years the Prince of Wales had stayed for the St Leger with Christopher Sykes at his home Brantingham Thorpe. But by 1890 Sykes was on the verge of bankruptcy and in that year the Prince was informed that Sykes would not be able to entertain him in the accustomed fashion. As a result he was forced to stay in a strange house, Tranby Croft, something he never enjoyed doing, with a *nouveau riche* shipping magnate named Arthur

Wilson. The ostentatious, Italianate architecture of the industrialist's recently built home was a sign of the lack of any sort of taste his whole family were soon to show. The visit got off to an unpropitious start for His Royal Highness. He had planned to alleviate some of the inconvenience to which he had been put by having his current favourite, Daisy Brooke, in the house party. But at the last moment she was unable to attend because of the death of her step-father, the Earl of Rosslyn. Despite this loss, the Prince ensured that he was accompanied by a number of his friends and racing acquaintances including Reuben Sassoon, Lord Edward Somerset, the Earl of Coventry and his wife, and General Owen Williams. Also in the party was Sir William Gordon Cumming. In his mid–forties, a baronet, a Lieutenant-Colonel in the Scots Guards, rich, good-looking and a friend of the Prince of Wales, Gordon Cumming had seemingly impeccable qualifications for success in Society. He

Sir William Gordon Cumming by Ape.

also had a certain arrogance which made him unpopular with many people. As one contemporary put it, 'He had cuckolded so many husbands and been witty at the expense of so many fools.'

Having attended the first day of the race meeting the house party returned to Tranby Croft. After dinner the Prince of Wales suggested a game of baccarat. He supplied the counters marked with his Prince of Wales's crest and motto. It was known to some members of the party that the parvenu, Mr Wilson, did not approve of baccarat. However, he could hardly complain if the suggestion had come from the Prince himself. Such a move would have seriously jeopardized his family's chances of social elevation – certainly a high priority in the ambitious Mrs Wilson's mind, whose father was a postmaster in Leeds.

While the play was in progress with the Prince of Wales as banker, Wilson's son, also Arthur, thought that he saw Sir William cheating – by adding counters to his stake after the allowed time, and if he thought that he was going to win the hand. After his initial disbelief young Wilson informed his neighbour, Berkeley Levitt, a Captain in the Scots Guards, that Sir William was cheating. At first Levitt did not believe him, particularly as the man accused was a Colonel in his regiment. But having watched Sir William for some time Levitt also became convinced. After the game had finished and the guests retired to bed, the headstrong Wilson told Levitt that he was going to inform his brother-in-law, Lycett Green, a stupid and pushy young man, married to the Wilson's daughter, Ethel. In fact he did not tell Lycett Green that night, but went instead to his mother. Her initial reaction was horror at the possible scandal in her house. It seems that neither she nor her son informed Mr Wilson at that stage. The next morning, however, young Wilson foolishly told Lycett Green, who told his wife.

The party again spent the day at the races, the Prince and his friends, including Sir William, totally unaware of the disaster that was brewing. As it was likely that the Prince would wish to play baccarat again that evening Mrs Wilson, her son and Lycett Green had decided to watch Sir William's game and then take steps – what steps they were not certain. They also ensured that the butler produced a proper card-table for the evening rather than the makeshift arrangement they had had on the first night. As expected, the Prince did wish to play baccarat again. It was during that second evening's play that the Wilson family group, who were later to be Sir William's accusers in court, were all convinced that he was indeed cheating. They took no steps that evening; certainly Mrs Wilson for one was dreading the consequences, whatever the outcome. It seemed that all her illusions of grandeur were on

The scene of the crime: the card table in the billiard room at Tranby Croft.

the verge of ruin. The next morning Lycett Green took the first step in revealing the affair by telling Lord Edward Somerset. The latter was obviously astonished, but was forced to listen to their accusations. Rather than make any judgement himself he told them to go and see Lord Coventry. The Earl of Coventry was, after the Prince himself, the senior member of the party. By now the Wilson group had, unwittingly, ensured not only Sir William's downfall, but also their own.

Once again they all had the day's racing to think about the problem but when the party returned to Tranby Croft, matters came swiftly to head. Lycett Green, who had become self-appointed spokesman for the accusers, repeated his story to Lord Coventry and General Owen Williams. Together they went straight to the Prince and told him. The Prince was naturally horrified – mainly at the possible implications and scandal that could be attached to his name – as baccarat was the subject of widespread disapproval. It was then that the three men discussed the possibility of drawing up a document for Sir William to sign by which he would promise to refrain from

playing cards for the rest of his life. The next step was to confront Sir William himself, which Lord Coventry and General Williams duly did.

Not surprisingly, Sir William vehemently denied the charge and demanded to see the Prince. When he did so it seemed that the Prince took the evidence of five accusers as something that Sir William could not disprove. For when Sir William again protested his innocence the Prince replied: 'What can you do, there are five accusers against you?' Sir William's reply was that he would publicly insult the five at the first possible opportunity. The Prince only told him bluntly that it would do no good. As with Lord Coventry and General Williams, Sir William ended by asking, 'What am I to do?' For the time being no one ventured to tell him, but after the Prince had interviewed Berkeley Levitt, Lycett Green and young Wilson, the course of action was determined. A document was drawn up, probably by Lord Coventry, which Sir William was to sign. It not only demanded an oath to refrain from gambling, but, as Sir William protested, was tantamount to an admission of guilt. His first reaction was to tell them that he would not sign and would go to his commanding officer. When they pointed out that the senior soldier was less likely to be so lenient and the alternative to signing was to leave the house immediately and face being warned off the Turf, he gave in and signed. In return they, and all those at the house party were sworn to secrecy. The Prince of Wales's signature was, with the other leading members of the affair, added to the document. With not a little trepidation they all fervently hoped that it would be the last they would hear of the scandal.

Whether in fact the story had got out (leaked one day at the races by one of the house party), before they were all sworn to secrecy, was not discovered

Doncaster racecourse: where the story got out.

*Daisy Brooke – 'Lady Babblebrook' – blamed with
spreading the story of Tranby Croft.*

but it seems highly likely. However dangerous the situation, such an outrageous piece of gossip would have been irresistable, particularly to one of Sir William's enemies. Whenever it did escape it was well known before Christmas 1890 that the story of Sir William's alleged cheating was becoming increasingly widely circulated among members of Society. Many people thought that the Prince himself had told Lady Brooke and that she was responsible for the story going on general release. As a result one wit nicknamed her Lady 'Babblebrook'. However the story got out it was becoming increasingly clear to Sir William that he was going to have to take some steps to clear his name. On 6 February 1891 he instigated an action for slander against the five people who had accused him and claimed £5,000 damages. But before the case got into court there was a flurry of activity to prevent it doing so – largely at the request of the Prince of Wales. After the unpleasantness of the Mordaunt Affair he had no wish to be subjected to having to appear in the witness-box again. Far more serious were the possible consequences, for his reputation and that of the monarchy, of his name being involved in such a scandal.

In the event, what happened must have far exceeded his worst fears. As news of the impending case became common knowledge Members of Parliament, the Church and the Press, as well as other sundry high-minded individuals, seized their God-given opportunity and leapt to the attack. The criticism soon reached fever-pitch, with radicals denouncing the monarchy and others contenting themselves with giving the Prince of Wales and his racing friends the roughest few months of their lives. One contemporary described the religious publications as, 'great moral elephants, trumpeting their horror and piously running amok.' The note of hysteria which crept into the accusations against racing and gambling is clearly shown by the outcry from one vicar in an article:

> Do you know what goes on in Doncaster during the great race-week in early September? Importation of scores of prostitutes, immigration of scores of practical thieves, thimble-riggers, pick-pockets, gamblers and cheats of every description, liquor shops open at night, houses of ill-fame all open, drinking, cursing, swearing and fighting; in plain words 'Hell broke loose in the slums of Doncaster'.

Cartoons, particularly of the Prince playing cards were rife; one of the favourites carried the caption 'Ich Deal' making a play on the Prince's motto 'Ich Dien'. People were particularly outraged when they heard that the baccarat had been played with counters supplied by the Prince.

When the case came up for trial it was probably the most sensational of Queen Victoria's (or Edward VII's) reign. It was heard in the Lord Chief Justice's Court in front of Lord Coleridge himself. The five accused by Sir William were represented by Sir Charles Russell, who had defended Lord Durham, aided by George Lewis – it was inconceivable that the society solicitor would not be active in the most sensational society case of his life. Sir William's council was Sir Edward Clarke, the Solicitor-General and probably the most brilliant advocate of his day.

The hearing began on 1 June and throughout Clarke's handling of the proceedings was extremely adroit. It was not long before he had the general opinion of the court solidly behind Sir William. Even the Prince of Wales was not exempt from Clarke's scathing remarks. To the fury of His Royal Highness – who had initially been relieved when he heard that Clarke was acting for Sir William, believing that the Solicitor-General would help bring proceedings to a rapid end – he had to listen to the legal expert maintain that Sir William had been victimized to save the face of the Prince, that he himself was at fault for having initiated the game of baccarat and that he had ignored 'Queen's Regulations'. (It was stated in army regulations that any case where

PALL MALL BUDGET. JUNE 11, 1891

THE BACCARAT TRIAL

"WAITING FOR THE ACCUSED." (With all acknowledgments to the Hon J. Collier)

I confess that I attach very little importance to Sir William having signed a document which was tantamount to an admission of the truth of the charge. The scene reminds me of what must often have occurred in the dungeons of the Inquisition. "Recant, or——." And often the victim did recant. Suddenly they burst in upon him whilst he was dressing for dinner. He denied the charge indignantly. They used the "utmost pressure" to force him to sign. They gave him to understand that, if only he would sign, the whole business would remain a secret for ever. MR. LABOUCHERE in *Truth.*

*One of the host of cartoons which appeared lampooning the Prince of Wales –
and, in this case, his motto.*

an officer's conduct or honour had been impugned in public must be reported
for military investigation). Clarke went on to argue that the Prince of Wales
and General Owen Williams were the only two experienced baccarat players
in the party at Tranby Croft and yet neither had suspected anything about
Sir William's play until it was brought to their attention. In contrast, Sir
William's accusers – especially Lycett Green, who was soon to regret his
outspokenness – were to reveal a lamentable ignorance of the game, on the
basis of which they had seen fit to take action. Green's wife even had the
effrontery to admit that it was Sir William who had taught her how to play
baccarat.

Clarke was, however, up against formidable odds, not least the personal
animosity of Lord Coleridge which Clarke afterwards maintained caused the

Sir William Gordon Cumming in the witness-box.

Lord Chief Justice to influence the jury in his summing up. Lord Coleridge also made certain that Clarke was not able to subject the Prince of Wales to detailed cross-examination. In the end, it was the Prince's reply to a question by a member of the jury which largely decided their final verdict. The man asked, 'Did your Royal Highness observe anything in the plays of Sir William Gordon Cumming on either of the nights that was suspicious?' 'No I did not', His Royal Highness replied, 'We were playing in a country house among friends. I was busy, acting as banker, and had no suspicion of such a thing.' The man seizing his brief moment of glory, continued by asking the Prince's opinion of the charge made against Sir William at the time. The Prince replied, 'The charges seemed so unanimous that there was no course open but to believe them.' Whatever their opinions of His Royal Highness, the fact that the Prince had not seen any possibility of disbelieving the charges, dearly though he would have loved to have done so, greatly influenced the jury. Added to this was Lord Coleridge's demand that they consider only the question of Sir William's cheating – thus averting the chance of any undue attention being focussed on the possibly dubious motives of the five defendants.

The tide might have turned against Sir Edward Clarke but he had spared no effort in his condemnation of Sir William's accusers and most members of the party involved. When he accused Lord Coventry and General Williams of acting to prevent the Prince's name being involved in a scandal, and insinuated that they had made Sir William a scapegoat, cheering broke out in the public gallery. After six days in court the Prince had had enough and on the final day – when the jury announced their verdict – he was at Ascot, where the boos of the crowd were the final insult. Sir Edward Clarke's valient efforts had been to no avail and the jury returned in favour of the five defendants. The verdict was greeted in court with a round of hisses, for by this time Sir William had gained widespread support.

Despite the public sympathy, and the fact that he was almost certainly innocent, he was a ruined man. Shortly after the case the *Official Gazette* announced that his name had been taken off the list of serving officers, tersely giving the reason that, 'Her Majesty has no further occasion for his services.' He was ostracised from Society for the rest of his life and it can only have been small comfort that the day after the trial he married an American heiress, Florence Garner. The Prince of Wales referred to his marriage as, 'the crowning point of his infamy', and Sir William and his wife spent the rest of their lives in isolation at his Scottish seat, Gordonstoun. (Ironically Gordonstoun was later to become a school established along lines of strict morality and the *alma mater* of the present Prince of Wales.)

Sir William might have gained a grain of satisfaction from the knowledge that the downfall of the Wilson family was as complete as his own. Their inability to conduct themselves with the sort of discretion expected of members of society shattered any illusions they may have held about the possible rewards of their home's brief elevation. Instead they were banished into obscurity.

The Prince of Wales may not have been ruined, but he emerged from the affair severely battered. He had been hauled over the coals by almost every single English newspaper and by numerous ones abroad. Equally intolerable, he had suffered the ignominy of being told by his least favourite nephew, the Kaiser, that he strongly disapproved of his uncle being involved in such a scandal. As well as the personal blows to his reputation, he had been forced to endure six upleasant days in court including being closely cross-examined as a witness.

The gross impositions did not end with the court's verdict. A group of the stuffier variety of society ladies and dowagers felt that the Prince was getting off too lightly. A number of them, who strongly disapproved of his lifestyle – in particular his racing and card-playing – had in the past been frustrated by

Mrs Wilson being cross-examined.

the lack of an opportunity to take him to task. They now lost no time in laying most of the blame for the sordid events and publicity of the Tranby Croft firmly at his door. Having made their feelings known to Queen Victoria they then approached the Archbishop of Canterbury. Victoria had been horrified by the scandal but objected to being told how she should deal with her son. Archbishop Benson, however, was agreeable to the ladies' suggestion that he should write a letter to the Prince, asking him to denounce gambling and those people who indulged in it, and that the Prince's reply should be in the form of an open letter to be published in *The Times*. At first the Prince flatly refused to co-operate, arguing that such a letter would only make hypocrisy another of the charges that the public would be able to hurl at him. Under strong pressure he eventually agreed. In his letter he wrote that he had a horror of gambling and went on to say, 'I consider gambling, like intemperance, one of the greatest curses that a country can be afflicted with.' He did, however, take the opportunity to condemn the Press for their totally unjust attacks – knowing that he was unable to defend himself – and to deplore the general abuse to which he had been subjected. He ended with what was, in the circumstances, a spirited defence of racing. 'Horse-racing may produce gambling or it may not. I have always looked upon it as a manly sport which is popular with Englishmen of all classes, and there is no reason why it should be looked on as a gambling transaction.' They were not exactly sentiments that his mother or the dowagers would have wished to hear.

It was some years before the Prince's prestige was restored and the hostility towards racing subsided. The near-fatal attack of typhoid which Prince George suffered and the death of the Prince of Wales's eldest son, Albert Victor Duke of Clarence, a year later, brought a wave of public sympathy. In the end, Persimmon's victory in the Derby in 1896 was the decisive factor in the restoration of the Prince's and the Turf's popularity. Public hostility became warm indulgence and Lord Granville was able to write, 'The Prince of Wales is loved because he has all the faults of which an Englishman is accused.'

The Mate, the Squire, the Sporting Earl and Colonel Harry

Scandals such as the Chetwynd v Durham libel and the Tranby Croft Affair had a disastrous effect on racing. There were, however, certain figures whose reputations and the general affection with which they were regarded, on and off the course, were a great bonus. One of the most popular – and one of the poorest – was Sir John Astley, 'The Mate'. Once he had retired from the army the Mate devoted himself to sport in general and racing in particular. His unmistakable figure, with a thick shock of hair and beard, was one of the best known on the Turf. His popularity notwithstanding, right up to his death, in 1894, his career was a constant struggle against the threat of financial disaster. At the end of 1883 he glumly recorded in his betting book at the end of that year, 'Am dead broke, shall have to live at Elsham like a blooming maggot in a nut. Shall I ever bet a monkey on a race again?'

The Mate embarked on his racing career with the vain hope of improving his finances. He never owned a great many horses, normally because he could not afford to buy them and was often forced to sell the ones he had to meet his debts. One year one of his best horses, Ostregor, was due to run in the Chesterfield Cup at Goodwood, but at the time Sir John's stable had been having a bad run. Into the bargain he owed £3,000 to Henry Padwick, supposedly a moneylender but with little doubt one of the worst crooks to frequent the racing world of the nineteenth century, and largely responsible for the downfall of the pathetic Marquess of Hastings among others. Shortly before Ostregor's race Sir John was approached by two officers of the Austrian army who offered him £3,000 for the horse, and he could do little but accept. When Ostregor won the Cup easily Sir John won £5,000 with a bet, but not even the offer of an extra £1,000 could buy his horse back as it was destined for the Austrian Emperor.

Probably the best horse the Mate owned was Peter, bought in 1881, but again due to ill fortune he only managed to keep him for a year. When Peter was beaten in the Manchester Cup the Mate lost £12,000. It was a mortal blow. Trying to make amends he ran Peter in the Queen's Vase at Royal Ascot, but the horse's uncertain temperament got the better of him and he pulled up halfway through the race. The next day he ran in the Hunt Cup,

The Mate, Sir John Astley, contemplating his luck.

The Mate, striking a characteristic pose in the centre of a group in front of Wynyard Park, the Londonderry seat.

Sir John having booked Fred Archer to ride him instead of Charlie Wood. At last Peter showed his true form by winning comfortably. With Archer riding him again he added to his success by winning the Hardwicke Stakes two days later but it was not enough to make up for the disaster of the Manchester Cup and by the autumn the Mate was forced to sell him for £6,000 – less than he had originally paid for the horse.

That year the Mate's horses ran 261 times and not only did they achieve 64 wins, but they were in the first three 149 times. He won £16,800 in bets and £15,871 in stakes but was, in his own words, 'cruel hard-up'.

By 1883 he had sold all his horses and despite winning £26,968 in bets over twenty-six years had nothing to show for it. Undismayed, the Mate accepted the situation: ' . . .Well my ability was *not* superior, that is certain; and so I continued spending when I won, and borrowing when I lost, till at last I had to pull up, and eke out the rest of my days, as I am now doing, on a small allowance.'

Despite his almost full-time involvement in racing Sir John was, for a short time, a Member of Parliament. As he conceded, it was an unexpected move, 'I now became a Legislator – oh dear! Was there ever such a parody on that exalted title.' What he lacked in political knowledge he often made up for with his jovial repartee. At a meeting where he was canvassing shortly before his election, the Mate was asked by a studious-looking member of the audience what he thought of Sir Wilfred Lawson's 'Liquor Bill'. 'To tell you the truth I don't know much about Sir W. Lawson's Liquor Bill, but I do know that mine was a damned sight too high this year.' He did successfully introduce a Bill to Parliament, making it a punishable offence for men to poison cart-horses, apparently a matter of some concern in his rural Lincolnshire constituency. He was better known for a number of outspoken statements such as when he announced that he had never met under one roof, forty or more confounded rascals than Ireland had sent up to represent Her Majesty in the House of Commons. When he failed to be re-elected at the 1880 General Election the Mate was as relieved as many of his constituents – who returned a Radical.

The Mate's administrative skills were more evident as a member of the Jockey Club and he was one of the three stewards when the rules of racing were redrafted during the 1870s. At the same time a serious case of fraud – known as the Sphinx Fraud – was uncovered. Three men had bought a mare called Sphinx and were entering her in races under a different name and at the wrong age. The men came up in front of a tribunal of the Jockey Club stewards. During the tribunal, the other two stewards – Admiral Rous who

was virtually deaf, and Lord Hardwicke – spent most of the time asleep and snoring loudly. Lord Hardwicke only woke up briefly to tell one of the accused that he was, 'a villain of the deepest dye', for which he was roundly abused by the victim. The trio eventually went before a judge and got varying sentences of hard labour for their crimes. More important was the Mate's supervision of the building of a new stand on Newmarket racecourse. The old one that it replaced had been so unsafe Sir John marvelled that the members of the Jockey Club had escaped serious injury.

Much of the Mate's popularity stemmed from his compulsive generosity, particularly towards stable lads whose mean existence was largely ignored by most other patrons of the Turf. On one occasion he saved the life of a boy who was thrown off a horse and had his leg amputated as a result of his injuries. Sir John collected a fund for him and eventually employed the boy to help him with his splendidly robust autobiography, *Fifty Years of my Life*, which the Mate produced in an attempt to alleviate his shortage of money.

If the Mate was racing's most popular figure towards the end of the nineteenth century, certainly the most unpopular was George Alexander Baird, known to his cronies as 'The Squire'. Baird came from a Scottish family who had made a fortune in coal and iron. Before he was ten he had inherited from his father and uncle a combined fortune of over £3 million. His widowed mother was quite incapable of controlling him and although he went to both Eton and Cambridge he left without the vestige of an education. The only pastime he had been interested in was hunting, and shortly after coming into his money he embarked on a career in racing, primarily as a gentleman rider. Not only did his unruly behaviour bring him into disrepute, but also his rough riding tactics were widely criticized. Two years after registering his colours in 1880, his supposed threat to Lord Harrington to, 'shove him over the rails', was brought to the attention of the stewards of the Jockey Club who had no hesitation in warning him off for two years. It was an inauspicious start.

When able to return Baird was determined to prove himself by acquiring a first-class string of horses and riding as many winners as possible. He could afford to buy virtually what he wanted and at the dispersal sale of Lord Falmouth's horses in 1884 his total bill of over £17,000 was by far the largest of any single buyer. His purchases included an outstanding three-year-old filly called Busybody who shortly afterwards won the One Thousand Guineas and the Oaks. But neither the racing authorities nor Society were prepared to be forgiving; the two victories were greeted without a murmur of

congratulation. As a result Baird's ambitions as an owner became secondary to his career as a rider, when he competed under the assumed name of 'Mr Abington' to avoid being discovered by his trustees. More dangerous, it made him bitterly resentful and determined never to temper his behaviour to what was socially acceptable.

Most of the time it was utterly the reverse. With characteristic weakness Baird surrounded himself with a crowd of the most unsavoury characters imaginable, most of whom were primarily interested in getting their hands on as much of his money as they could; not a difficult task as Baird was a compulsive spendthrift. Most of them came from the seamy side of prize-fighting which Baird supported keenly. While he was quite happy to be taken in by their flattery they could hardly believe their luck. The Squire established his stables at Bedford Lodge in Newmarket, and one of his first improvements was to build a boxing saloon on one side of the house. Here Baird and his cronies spent days on end in drunken stupors, emerging at intervals to watch a bout, a cock-fight or a dog-fight – in which Baird's bull-terrier Donald was normally one of the protagonists. Meanwhile the luckless Martin Gurry, the first of Baird's string of private trainers, had the task of looking after his horses.

Surprisingly enough, though, Baird showed remarkable dedication to his riding. Even after a week-long drinking spree he would be up at dawn working his horses and his record of wins as a gentleman rider was scarcely rivalled by any of his contemporaries. He would go to any lengths to ride a winner – on one occasion he hired a whole train so that it would take him to one of the more out-of-the-way northern courses where he wanted to ride a favourite in a seller – but he shunned the main meetings where he would have to mix with the people who had turned their backs on him.

Baird was almost totally taboo in houses belonging to any member of society or anyone with a respectable reputation in racing. Exceptions were few and Sir George Chetwynd, who was one, did not hold onto his house for very long. Baird was dining with Sir George at his London home in Curzon Street at a time when the baronet was particularly hard up. When the Squire voiced his admiration for his surroundings Sir George quickly replied that it was all for sale, at the right price. It was too much for Baird to resist and, making an offer of £15,000, which Sir George could not refuse he took possession of the house and all its contents there and then. That night Sir George left – to go where history does not relate – and Baird retired to his new sleeping quarters. The next morning he had to be remained where he was when, somewhat alarmed and undoubtedly hung over, he asked his whereabouts: 'At home, Squire', one of his prize-fighting acolytes replied.

The Squire; never happier than when riding a winner. By Lib.

Lillie Langtry, who received many bruises and many thousands of pounds from the Squire.

Despite displaying little interest in his horses, unless they were ones he was able to ride, Baird did own a number of good animals. His greatest success was in 1887 when he won the Derby with a horse called Merry Hampton. Even then, his resentful pride prevented him from gaining any enjoyment from racing's supreme prize, as Richard Onslow described in his biography of Baird, *The Squire*:

> As Jack Watts brought Merry Hampton back to the winner's enclosure, everyone waited to see how the *enfant terrible* of the Turf would greet the horse that had brought him the triumph many other millionaires had sought in vain for half a lifetime or more. But to the utter amazement of those who could see him, the Squire, not generally remarkable for his reserve or unemotional nature, was lounging against the rails, taking not the slightest interest in proceedings . . .

The Squire was clearly not going to give people the opportunity of ignoring him again, as they had when Busybody had won the Oaks.

The best horse the Squire ever owned was Gallinule. Ironically, having paid an enormous price for the animal, he then could not wait to get rid of it at any price. He bought Gallinule for £5,000 at the sale of the erratic 4th Marquess of Aylesbury's horses in 1887. The Marquess, known as 'Billy Stomachache', was a boorish oaf whose stupidity had got him into bad hands and landed him in trouble with the authorities. His horses were being sold as a result of him being warned off. What the Squire did not know at the time was that Gallinule, a huge horse of bull-like appearance, had a tendency to burst blood vessels which seriously hampered what could have been an outstanding racing career. Early in 1889 he had improved enough to be entered in the Lincolnshire Handicap and Baird and his friends piled on their money. When Gallinule broke another blood vessel and finished unplaced it was the final straw in a very expensive enterprise. The Squire – furiously blaming everyone but himself – was determined to get rid of the horse as soon as possible. He was sold to a young officer for £900. In years to come Gallinule sired the winners of 663 races worth £316,963, including Pretty Polly, one of the greatest fillies of all time.

Among the exploits which least endeared him to his contemporaries, Baird was a compulsive womanizer and displayed none of the accepted niceties in pursuit of his prey. Although 'Billy Stomachache' had at one time enjoyed Baird's company, the main reason why he saw no reason to warn Baird of Gallinule's shortcomings was because the Squire had once kidnapped his wife. The kidnap had been in revenge for Lady Aylesbury – originally a working-class actress called Dolly Tester, and at one time Baird's mistress – having made off with a selection of jewellery which the Squire had sent her to choose one piece from.

His most notorious affair – with Lillie Langtry – began in 1891. By the end of the 1880s Lillie had ceased to be the Prince of Wales's mistress. She was intrigued by Baird's reputation and greatly attracted by his money – of which she was perpetually short. Baird lavished thousands on her and bought her her first racehorses. Their affair was torrid and bizarre. One Sunday when she was not on stage at the Haymarket Theatre Lillie was summoned urgently to find the Squire and friends indulging in a rat-catching competition with two dogs in the foyer. More unpleasant, Baird subjected her to the physical violence with which he was always reputed to have treated his mistresses. Lillie's candid reply when asked why she allowed him to inflict such terrible bruises was, 'I detest him, but every time he does it he gives me a cheque for £5,000.' The climax came when she went off to Paris for the weekend with another man. Enraged with jealousy Baird followed her to her hotel and beat

her up so badly that she ended up in hospital. Even so, relations were restored when Baird gave her a cheque for £50,000 and a yacht called the 'White Lady' for which he paid £20,000 in cash. The boat was commonly known as the 'Black Eye'.

There was an air of inevitability about Baird's short but self-destructive career. When the end came it was both pathetic and unimpressive. The grasping people with whom he surrounded himself were always as much of an enemy as any of his personal failings and they brought his final downfall. During the winter of 1892 they persuaded him to accompany them to America to put up the money for a bout for the heavyweight title of the world between Charlie Mitchell, a regular of Baird's circle and a prize-fighter of some repute, and 'Gentleman Jim' Corbett, the American champion. It was ironic that at the end of 1892 Baird had one of the best prospects for the Classics of 1893 in Meddler, who had won the prestigious Dewhurst Stakes at Newmarket as a two-year-old. He also showed signs of making a determined effort to end what had become a state of virtually permanent alcoholism and return to serious riding. His improvement was largely inspired by the influence of his latest and last trainer, Joe Cannon. But when the time came even Cannon could not prevent the Squire leaving for America — the trainer was barred from his London house by the boxing mob. In March 1893 the Squire contracted malarial fever as well as pneumonia while staying in New Orleans and was in no state to resist either disease as his drinking since he had arrived in America had been worse than ever. He died in a seedy hotel room and it was only through the intervention of the British Consul that his body was returned to England rather than being buried anonymously in America.

Like the Marquess of Hastings, to whom he showed frightening similarities for many people, Baird had squandered a huge fortune: over £2 million in just over ten years. Despite his manifold faults much of it was due to compulsive generosity – albeit normally to the benefit of totally unsuitable people. But with his will he had the last word and surprised both his enemies and so-called friends. The residue of his fortune – amazingly still hardly less than £1 million – was left to his mother who had brought him up and had been the only person to whom he had shown unfailing affection throughout his turbulent life.

Another man who, like the Squire, dissipated an enormous fortune through his own personal recklessness and extravagance, was Hugh Lowther, 5th Earl of Lonsdale. The Sporting Earl, the Yellow Earl, or just plain Lordy as he was variously addressed by all and sundry, was a larger-than-life figure. For Lord

Lord Lonsdale as a young man; about to embark on his spectacular spending spree.

Ancaster he was, 'almost an emperor and not quite a gentleman'. In contrast to Baird, who always remained a social outcast, by the end of his life Hugh had built up an extraordinary charisma. The mass of his contemporaries could forgive him anything because he was – by popular consent – England's

greatest sportsman. As a young man his shortage of money and uncontrollable wildness ensured that he was largely disapproved of by Society. But only six years after he had arrived at Lowther in a drunken stupor to take up his inheritance, the 4th Earl, St George, died suddenly and his younger brother Hugh inherited. As Graham Sutherland wrote in his biography, *The Yellow Earl*: 'Trumpeting like a thirsty bull elephant who suddenly scents water, he cut a swathe through Society – who never quite forgave him for it.' (Hugh may have conducted himself with more decorum when the guest of one of the railway companies, but whenever he travelled overnight *two* first-class sleeping compartments were reserved – one for His Lordship and one for his dogs.)

Shortly after his marriage to Lady Grace Gordon, the daughter of the Marquess of Huntly, his wife had an accident out hunting while she was pregnant. As well as losing her baby she was told that she could never have any children. Hugh was bitterly disappointed and although he had a younger brother who would inherit and perpetuate the name, behaved from then on as though he was the last of the Lowthers. His incredible extravagance knew no bounds and was quite disastrous. Before he inherited Hugh had sold his right of reversion to raise some cash and as a result, although he was one of the richest men in England, was under the control of his trustees. Like a number of similarly hampered aristocrats, Hugh saw life as a series of campaigns against the trustees. His cousin and senior trustee, James ('Jim') Lowther, a distinguished politician and member of the Jockey Club, was the only man who had any control over Hugh. When he died in 1904 there was no one who could stem the tide of spending.

One can hardly believe that the expenditure had to be controlled, considering that when he became Earl of Lonsdale, Hugh's income from the family estates, coal and iron mines was roughly £4,000 per week, which gave him £80–100,000 to spend per annum – between £2.8 and £3½ million today. And yet only three years after his brother's death Jim Lowther was forced to apply sanctions for the first of many times. The lifestyle of the Sporting Earl was quite spectacular. It became a personal obsession that he had to have the best and the most of everything. While St George lay on his deathbed his younger brother sat waiting patiently in the next room smoking endless cigarettes. Hugh had never liked his brother, being obsessively jealous of his wealth as the son and heir, his string of racehorses and his marriage to one of the most beautiful women of the day. They were the last cigarettes he ever smoked: from the moment he inherited only specially made six-inch cigars – called Lonsdales – were good enough for Hugh. For the rest of his life he was

never seen without one jutting from his mouth; they alone cost him about £3,000 per year.

Hugh's racing colours were bright canary yellow, a shade which liberally adorned all his possessions. The famous fleet of Lonsdale carriages were painted bright yellow, as were later his replacement fleet of cars, and his scores of servants wore similarly striking livery. As one of his footmen once remarked, 'I believe that if he could have painted *us* yellow he'd have done it.' Horses were of foremost importance in his life and he had to have the best – at any price. In fact it was his hunting expenses and carriage horses which were a major drain on his resources rather than racehorses.

Even the Lowther fortunes could not sustain the tide. Well before the end of Hugh's life the progressive sales of property began; Whitehaven Castle, Barleythorpe, the enormous hunting-box in Rutland, Carlton House Terrace in London (in fact two mansions joined together). Eventually Lowther Castle itself was closed and Hugh went to ground at Stud House near Barleythorpe. In 1898, after six disastrously expensive years as Master of the Quorn, Jim Lowther forced him to both resign as Master and sell the majority of the enormous string of horses he had built up. At the sale, eighty-four horses fetched a total of £18,228. A spectator remarked, 'They must think they are buying bloody racehorses.'

Hugh's early education was entrusted by his father first to his old batman, who had been the regimental heavyweight boxing champion, and later to Jem Mace, the champion bare-fist fighter. It was hardly likely to encourage discipline or any love of learning. As Hugh was let loose on the world the unacceptably outrageous nature of many of his antics greatly upset Society. One notorious incident occurred in the most public place in London – Hyde Park during the fashionable hour for Society's parade. During the 1880s Hugh had been competing with Sir George Chetwynd for the favours of Lillie Langtry, and it was she who brought the rivalry to its unseemly climax. While riding with Hugh, she stopped to talk to Sir George and the two men confronted each other. It seems that Sir George demanded: 'Don't meddle with my Lillie!' and at the same time struck Hugh with his whip. Hugh responded in a similar manner and as their horses became uncontrollable in the ensuing mêlée both men dismounted to continue the fight with their fists. Eventually, rolling in the dirt and liberally spattered with blood, they were dragged apart by the Duke of Portland and Sir William Gordon Cumming. The newspapers and general public lapped it up but Society was outraged.

As he got older, and through the steadying influence of his wife, Hugh's wildness abated and his notoriety became less tainted fame. Boxing remained

Lord Lonsdale (centre) admires a runner at Ascot.

one of his favourite pastimes for the rest of his life and, apart from the Marquess of Queensberry, he is the best-known figure in the sport's history. He was largely responsible for giving the sport some sort of respectability, and presented the magnificent Lonsdale belts. But it was at the races that the sporting Earl went on public display and by the end of the century he was probably the best-known figure on the racecourse after the Prince of Wales. It became a tradition at Royal Ascot that Lord Lonsdale drove down the course behind the royal party on the opening day in his yellow carriages which put the more subdued royal landaus slightly in the shade. When he became Senior Steward of the Jockey Club it was an excuse for another bout

Harry McCalmont: the Squire of Cheveley.

Cheveley Park under construction, with the works' steam train in front of the house.

of lavish entertainment: for weeks before the Derby the servants at Lowther were out scouring the fields for plovers' eggs to be served in his private box.

It is perhaps surprising that Lord Lonsdale did not gamble; he stopped for good after one night in his youth when he lost £18,000 in the evening playing cards at the Duke of Devonshire's house in Newmarket. Hugh was quite incapable of finding that sort of money and yet it was socially impossible for him to default on the debt. In the end Lord Calthorpe, an old family friend, baled him out on condition that Hugh promised never to gamble again.

As a private individual Hugh never had many horses in training. During the First World War, Colonel Hall-Walker sold or gave all his horses to the government, thus providing the foundation of the National Stud. The Ministry of Agriculture looked for a candidate to manage the horses' and their racing careers and they chose Lord Lonsdale. When asked in the House of Commons about the horses, 'Whose colours will they run in – the Coalition's or the Prime Minister's?' the Under-Secretary for War replied 'Lord Lonsdale's'. It was almost unanimously popular and Hugh took to his new role as a leading owner with gusto.

One of the few ambitions that Hugh never achieved was to become Master of the Horse, one of the Great Officers of the Realm. It was a possibility more than once, but as King George V remarked sadly, 'I should really like to have Hugh, the only trouble is that I could never afford him.' In his spending, the sartorial elegance of his appearance and in the scale of his existence there was probably no one who could compete with the Earl of Lonsdale. His extravagance which sent his family's fortunes plummeting would have appalled both his predecessors and his descendants whom he left in considerably reduced circumstances, when he died in 1944. All his life he was oblivious to criticism and constraints and his catchphrase was, 'It's all such lovely fun.'

There was nothing aristocratic about Colonel Harry McCalmont's background, but like Lord Lonsdale he showed an amazing alacrity for spending enormous amounts of money. Colonel Harry came into his fortune only fourteen years before his premature death, at the age of forty-one, in 1902. During those years he lived life on a lavish scale. Everything he owned: his houses, his yacht and his string of racehorses, was large. He inherited around £4 million from his great-uncle and by the time of his death had disposed of over half of it.

The McCalmont family originated from Scotland. Their fortune was founded in trade with the West Indies and late safeguarded and increased by the establishment of a family merchant bank. Harry was in the army when

he inherited but lost no time in taking advantage of his new-found largess. It was not long before he possessed a yacht, a house in St James's Square and had bought the Cheveley Park estate near Newmarket from the Duke of Rutland, whose family were not actively involved in racing. At the same time he commissioned Captain Machell, the well-known racing manager, to start buying racehorses for him.

Not content with the existing establishment at Cheveley Park, Colonel Harry pulled down the extensive old house and in a few years had erected a vast, Neo-Palladian mansion. No expense was spared and a miniature railway line with its own engine and trucks was put in to assist the builders with their construction. New stables were built in similarly impressive, classical style.

Colonel Harry's racing colours were scarlet and light blue quartered, the colours of the Eton football team, for which he had played with distinction. He did not have to wait long for his first successes. In 1892 he won the Royal Hunt Cup at Ascot with a horse called Suspender – suitably named considering its parentage – by Muncaster out of Garterless. Far more significant in that year were the victories of a two-year-old son of Isonomy, named Isinglass. The next year Isinglass confirmed his potential by winning the Triple Crown and it was the misfortune of another good horse, Ravensbury, to be second to him in all three Classics. Isinglass's triumphs put Harry McCalmont at the head of the list of winning owners – a remarkable achievement considering he had registered his colours only five years earlier – and he was there for a second consecutive year in 1894, when Isinglass won the Princess of Wales

Isinglass: winner of the Triple Crown and a record in prize money.

Stakes, the Eclipse Stakes and the Jockey Club Stakes. By the end of his career Isinglass had won £57,455, a phenomenal record which stood until 1952. Throughout his three-year-old career, Isinglass was hampered by extremely hard ground. It was largely through the expertise of Captain Machell and his trainer Jimmy Jewitt that he won the three Classics. It was not until the Eclipse the following year that he was able to race on softer ground. Before the race Jewitt confidently told a friend that Isinglass would prove his real quality in the race, which indeed he did, pulverizing a field including Ladas, the Derby winner of a few weeks earlier.

In 1895 Harry McCalmont realized one of his life's ambitions by becoming a Member of Parliament, suitably for the Cambridgeshire constituency that included Newmarket. The election was very close and his victory may have been due in no small part to his famous drive round the constituency on polling day, when, in just under twelve hours, he covered nearly ninety miles in a coach visiting the towns and villages of his constituency. His sudden death from a heart attack in 1902 deprived the racing world of one of its most expansive characters. Thanks to his energetic – if extravagant – patronage he had become, in the space of a few years, not only one of the most successful owners of the closing years of the nineteenth century, but also one of the Turf's most popular figures, regarded with affection by owners, trainers and jockeys alike. Despite marrying twice, Harry had no children and after his death his horses were sold, thus putting the seal on his short-lived but colourful career.

Cheveley Park complete; with perfect surroundings.

THE PROFESSIONALS

A family trio: the jockey brothers Charlie, Tom and Sammy Loates.

In the 1870s and 1880s some of the trainers and jockeys could look back to the days when many owners still called them 'training-grooms' and 'riding-grooms'. Although skilled at their specialised jobs they were often personal servants working for one man. By the beginning of the 1900s it was very different. Private trainers were a rarity and nobody had their own jockey. Newmarket had become firmly established as racing's headquarters with the other main training centres in the south on the downs of Berkshire, Sussex and Wiltshire, as they have been ever since. In the north, trainers no longer enjoyed a monopoly over their northern courses as easy transport from the south was made possible by the advent of the railways.

As for the jockeys, gone were the days of feudal patronage, as exemplified by the story of John Day and the Duke of Grafton. After Day had won two important races at one meeting he was informed that the Duke wished to see him. 'I have sent for you as I am going to make you a present for your good riding; there is a twenty-pound note for you, and I hope you will not waste it.' As their fees for riding steadily increased and, more particularly, the bonuses from grateful owners for winning, many of them retired from riding rich men – or at least potentially rich. Some went on to become trainers and throughout the period the circle of the most successful trainers and jockeys was fairly small, many of them being related. Two generations of the Cannon

family followed on from three generations of the Day family who had been trainers and jockeys since the beginning of the century (and their descendants were still involved in racing after the Second World War). There were the Dawson brothers and during the 1890s the Loates brothers were three of the leading jockeys. The family connections have carried on well beyond the end of the Edwardian period; todays's greatest jockey, Lester Piggott, is a great-nephew of two of the best jockeys at the turn of the century, 'Morny' and Kempton Cannon and the great-grandson of their father, Tom Cannon, one of the outstanding jockeys of the nineteenth century. That is on Piggott's father's side. His mother was the sister of Fred Rickaby and their father, another Fred, was also a jockey.

George Lambton and the Duke of Portland were in agreement that the years of the 1880s were the greatest in their lifetimes, and not only because of the horses and their races and the few noble aristocrats who owned them. It was also the decade of triumph for some of racing's best and most successful trainers and jockeys – notably John Porter and Mat Dawson, and George Fordham, Tom Cannon and Fred Archer. Any combination of these five men was hard to beat and throughout their careers the number of winners they achieved – in partnership or competition – was astonishing. Blessed with a regular flow of top-class horses the trainers developed their profession into a science. With most of the worst rough riding and the corruption gone, the jockeys were safe to concentrate on riding winners which they developed into an art. That is not to say they were not fiercely competitive. On one occasion at Newmarket Archer and Charlie Wood were up against an unknown jockey from the north called Griffiths. When Griffiths' horse seemed to be going too well for Archer's liking the latter had no hesitation in veering into it and squeezing the horse between himself and Wood. For once the underdog was up to the occasion. Having dealt with Wood, whom he nearly unseated in the process he then turned on Archer and gave the champion some of his own medicine by pushing him onto the rails. When Griffiths eventually won the trainer of Archer's horse was outraged and wanted to object but Archer sportingly refused: 'No I can't. I started it.'

John Porter was probably the most highly regarded trainer of his day. He was not related to any of his racing contemporaries but, as shown by his training at Kingsclere rather than Newmarket, he enjoyed his independence. During a career of nearly fifty years he trained the winners of over one thousand races, worth £720,000 in prize money. His owners were rarely dissatisfied and almost never voluntarily took their horses away from his stables. The Prince of Wales was one of the few who did so. Another was

Baron Hirsch, for whom Lord Marcus Beresford also acted as racing manager.

The Baron was an Hungarian Jew who had amassed a fortune of millions financing the building of railways in Turkey and the Balkans. His friendship with the Prince of Wales began partly as a result of the spectacular partridge shooting which the Baron could offer on his enormous estates in Hungary. Hirsch was normally the figure people cited when accusing the Prince of befriending socially undesirable Jewish financiers and industrialists. On one occasion when the Prince was on his way to shoot with the Baron, the Austrian ambassador complained vehemently that the visit was totally against protocol, as the Baron was not accepted at the Court of the Austro-Hungarian Empire. As usual the Prince was unabashed and unimpressed and went ahead with his trip as planned, for he certainly felt more at home with the Baron than most of the senile or reactionary figures who populated the Court of Vienna.

The Baron took up racing in England in memory of his only son who had died as a young man, and whose happiest hours had been spent racing in England. The decisive move in the Baron's career as an owner came when he paid the enormous sum of £5,500 for a yearling filly called La Flèche, bred at the royal stud at Hampton Court. La Flèche was a daughter of St Simon whose owner, the Duke of Portland, the Baron had to beat off in his efforts to gain the filly. She proved a sound investment, winning over £30,000 in prize-money, in twelve races. They included the One Thousand Guineas, the Oaks and the St Leger in 1892 – a feat only a handful of fillies have ever achieved. Almost more remarkable was the fact that she won the Oaks only two days after running in the Derby which she would have won but for the stupidity of her jockey, George Barrett, who allowed her to get hopelessly behind with no chance of catching the leaders. Like many of his ilk, the Baron's generosity towards charitable institutions was well known. At the end of 1892 (La Flèche's three-year-old season) his horses had won a total of £42,000. He divided the whole lot between various charities and the next year when he only won £7,500 he doubled it before handing the money over to be distributed.

Despite La Flèche's successes the Baron's horses left Kingsclere with the Prince of Wales's at the end of 1892, as a result of Lord Marcus's differences with Porter. They also went to Richard Marsh at Newmarket, but after one year the Baron wanted to return to Kingsclere. When Porter told him that, unfortunately, his yard was full, the Baron made the following proposition:

> 'If you are willing to sell, I will buy Kingsclere for £20,000. As my trainer I will pay you a salary of £1,000. Further I will place £100,000 in the bank,

which shall be at your absolute disposal for the purchase of bloodstock, and you shall have the sole management of my horses. Any boxes I do not fill you can use for horses belonging to other owners.'

It was a measure of Porter's independence that he had no hesitation in refusing the offer. The Prince of Wales and Baron Hirsch were rare exceptions and throughout his career Porter was patronized by the leading owners. The first was Sir Joseph Hawley, for whom he won over one hundred races. In the late-1870s he trained Isonomy for Frederick Gretton, a rich, but unattractive and greedy brewer from Glasgow. Isonomy only raced once as a three-

The racing farrier.

John Porter (on grey horse on left), supervising his string on the Berkshire downs.

year-old when he won the Cambridgeshire against a huge field. But as a four-
and five-year-old he was the best horse in England and established himself as
one of the greatest handicappers of all time. Isonomy was universally popular
and never more so than when he ran an outstanding race to win the Manchester
Cup as a five-year-old, when he was carrying 9 stone 12 pounds and giving
45 pounds to The Abbot who had been third in the Two Thousand Guineas.
It was also the occasion when Porter had one of his rare altercations with an
owner. Before the race, Gretton had asked him to tell Tom Cannon, the
jockey, that he stood to gain £1,000 if he won. Porter was offered nothing.
After the race he told Gretton's secretary, 'You can tell Mr Gretton that if I
am not treated the same as Tom Cannon he can take his horses away from
Kingsclere on Monday. I am sick of seeing the jockey get everything and the
trainer nothing.' Gretton paid up.

Whoever came before or after, Porter's partnership with the Duke of
Westminster was the most productive of his career. It was also one of the
most successful in racing history. They won 246 races worth nearly a quarter
of a million pounds. The Duke of Westminster went to Kingsclere in 1881,
after the career of his first Derby winner, Bend Or. Porter trained the other

three – Shotover, Ormonde and Flying Fox – as well as all his other winners. Porter himself admitted that after the Duke's death Kingsclere was never the same again. It was divine justice that such a trainer should have the privilege (as he was the first to appreciate it was) to train the great Ormonde. Porter's opinion of the horse was simply that he made the achievements of all others sink into comparative insignificance. Although he never saw a horse of Ormonde's class again, with Flying Fox he had the satisfaction of giving the Duke his second Triple Crown winner in the last year of his patron's life.

Ormonde and Flying Fox were not the only Triple Crown winners that Porter trained. In 1891 Common achieved the same distinction for the partnership of Sir Frederick Johnstone and Lord Alington who were, after the Duke of Westminster, Porter's most successful owners. Looking at the horse in the paddock before the Two Thousand Guineas Sir Frederick remarked rather scornfully, 'He seems to be well named,' but he changed his opinion when the horse had not only won the three Classics, but fetched his owners the then record price for any horse of £15,000 when sold to Sir Blundell Maple, the furniture magnate. Just before the St Leger, Johnstone and Alington had turned down an offer of £14,000 from the Austrian Government. When the horse became Sir Blundell's property they persisted with a telegram: 'Would you accept 20,000 guineas for Common? Wire reply.' Back went the short message: 'Thanks for offer. The English Turf requires Common's services. Money will not tempt me.' Sir Blundell could well afford such apparent swagger.

The only man who could claim to rival John Porter as a trainer was Mat Dawson. Although they achieved similarly impressive results their characters could not have been more different. In contrast to the quiet and unassuming Porter, Mat always enjoyed a good row. When the Duke of St Albans dared to query one or two items on his year's account the proud little Scotsman demanded to see the account and, in front of the astonished Duke, flung it on the fire – unpaid – with the rebuke, 'That will settle all your disputes Your Grace!' His pride did not interfere with his achievements. Mat trained his first Classic winner in 1858 and died in 1898. During those forty years he trained twenty-eight Classic winners, including six Derbys. As Lord Falmouth retired, the young Duke of Portland emerged to take over as Mat's leading owner and it was shortly after his arrival that they made the historic purchase of St Simon.

The rivalry of St Simon and Ormonde was never resolved but in 1886 the fiercely competitive Mat was convinced that in Minting he had a horse to

The arch-competitor:
Mat Dawson in old age.

Fred Archer: a genius horseman.

beat Ormonde in the Classics. Shortly before the Two Thousand Guineas the
two celebrated trainers met and, after looking at the two horses, Mat predicted
confidently: 'When the race is being run you will hear them shouting
Ormonde and Saraband home; but when they get into the Dip it will be
"Minting!" and nothing else. My horse will leave 'em all there, John, you'll
see.'

When Minting was beaten it was the greatest blow of Mat's life. He shut
himself up in his house for the rest of the week and refused to come out.
Accepting the inevitable he did not run Minting in the Derby, preferring to
take him to France where he won the Grand Prix de Paris. But he was in for

another blow the next year when Ormonde, by this time afflicted as a 'roarer', managed to beat Minting for the second time, in the Hardwicke Stakes at Royal Ascot.

In 1885 Mat Dawson was aged sixty-five and moved from Heath House to the village of Exning, planning to retire. But his owners had different ideas and continued to send him horses. Among his wins in the last thirteen years of his life were the Earl of Rosebery's two Derbys with Ladas and Sir Visto in 1895 and 1896. When he was an old man and unable to ride a hack or walk without a stick, the Jockey Club allowed Mat to drive onto the heath in a small brougham to watch his horses working.

Porter and Dawson may have been the two most successful trainers throughout the last quarter of the nineteenth century. Knowledge of their prowess was, however, largely limited to the racing world and their reputations pale into insignificance when compared to one of the few popular heroes of racing history, Fred Archer.

In *Men and Horses I Have Known*, George Lambton describes the first time he saw Archer, and goes on to give a revealing portrait of the legendary figure:

> The first time I ever saw Archer (I did not know him until the following year) was on my first visit to Newmarket in 1879. Of course, I had read in the papers of his marvellous feats, and I was naturally anxious to see the great jockey. At St Pancras Station I saw the Duke of Hamilton talking to a quiet, pale-looking young man, dressed in a dark suit and a black tie with a big pearl in it. I asked who it was. 'Why, that is Archer,' was the answer, much to my surprise, for he was quite unlike what I had pictured him to be.
>
> About 5ft 10in in height, with a wonderfully slim and graceful figure, and remarkably small hands and feet, there was even at that time the shadow of melancholy in his face which indicated a side to his nature never far absent even in his brightest days, and which was partly responsible for his tragic death. No one seeing him for the first time would have put him down as a jockey, or suspected that such tremendous energy lurked in that frail body. It was that untiring energy which was the secret of his great success, leaving no stone unturned to achieve the one object of his life, the winning of races.
>
> From the beginning of the racing season to the end, health, leisure and pleasure were sacrificed, walking nearer eleven stone than ten in the winter he was always ready for Lincoln and Liverpool riding 8st 10lb. He had a Turkish bath in his own house, and he used some medicine which went by the name of 'Archer's Mixture', prepared by a clever doctor in Newmarket called Wright. I tried it myself when I was riding races, and from my own experience I should say it was made of dynamite . . .

Taking him all round, Fred Archer was the greatest of all jockeys. Apprenticed to Matthew Dawson when he was eleven years old, it was not long before his master discovered that in this long-legged boy he had something out of the common. He was only seventeen when he won the Two Thousand Guineas for Lord Falmouth on Atlantic. From that time to the end of his life, at the age of twenty-nine, he was at the head of the winning jockeys. The number of races he won was astounding. In 1876, 209; 1877, 218; 1878, 229; 1879, 197; 1880, 120; 1881, 220; 1882, 210; 1883, 232; 1884, 241; 1885, 246; 1886 (the year of his death), 170. They included five victories in the Derby, four in the Oaks and six in the St Leger.

He had many great qualities. To begin with, marvellous hands and seat. I think it was Joe Cannon who once said, 'When you give Archer a leg-up he drops into the saddle, and in a moment he and the horse are as one; no pulling up or lengthening of stirrups, but away they go, complete confidence between man and horse . . .

Archer had a wonderful intuition regarding the character of any horse once he had been on his back, and knew how to get the most out of him. He had undaunted nerve and supreme confidence in himself without any atom of conceit. When he was beaten by a neck for a race he generally thought that if he had done just this or not done that he would have won, and that is how a good jockey can make himself into a great one . . .

Archer's spectacular career brought him enormous prestige. If he told an owner to let him ride a horse because he had seen it run and thought he could do better, they invariably did. And if he told them not to run a certain horse in a certain race they normally did not. It also brought him financial rewards far in excess of any other jockey of his time or for many years afterwards. If he was popular with owners and trainers for whom he rode, he was idolized by the public. 'Archer's Up' was for many men the guarantee of success and one of the most spectacular punters of the century, George Wales, who eventually ruined himself, would regularly have £5,000 on Archer regardless of which horse he was riding. Sometimes they showed their gratitude with more than words; when he won the St Leger on Dutch Oven, John Hammond, who won a fortune, gave him £10,000. Archer could rarely resist helping a punter who was down on his luck and many men were saved from disaster by a timely tip from the maestro. Archer himself was strongly motivated by financial gain, although by the time he died he had spent most of his money. One of the few people who was unimpressed by Archer's reputation was Mat Dawson, who referred to him as, 'that damned, long-legged, tin-scraping young devil.' When they were in Mat's yard at Heath House with the Duke of Portland the jockey was roundly reprimanded by the trainer: 'Archer,

Nellie Archer

mon, where are your manners? Are ye not going to open the gate for his Grace?'

In 1883 Archer married Mat Dawson's niece, Nellie. Although it marked the beginning of the happiest few months of his life it also marked his descent on the path of tragedy which was to culminate in his death three and a half years later.

At the beginning of 1884 Nellie had a son but the baby died within a few hours. Then towards the end of the year she had a daughter. Fred was away riding and heard the good news by telegram. But by the time he returned to Newmarket Nellie was dying and he arrived too late to speak to her again. It was a shattering blow. Archer had adored Nellie for, despite his fame and success, she had given him the only real happiness in his life. Too often the rigorous and debilitating pressures he subjected himself to and his almost unnatural single-mindedness took all the pleasure out of his achievements. He never recovered from Nellie's death although, at the time, it did not appear to affect his riding form. In 1885 he rode one of the best races of his life to

win the Derby on Melton. The next year he won again – on Ormonde, the best horse he ever rode.

By the end of 1886 the relentless wasting to keep down his weight was combining with his inner gloom to take its toll. When a friend remarked anxiously how ill he looked he received the depressing reply, 'Well if I look bad now what shall I look like next Wednesday, when I ride St Mirin in the Cambridgeshire?' For that race Archer had to get his weight down to 8st 6lbs or 8st 7lbs. At the same time his normal competitiveness had been replaced by constant pessimism. Just before the race he was heard to say, 'I have never ridden the winner of the Cambridgeshire and if I don't succeed this time I shall never try again.' In the event he lost by a short head after a superhuman effort.

It went from bad to worse. Archer became so weak that he missed a meeting at Lincoln – something he had not done in years. But a few days later he insisted on appearing at Brighton to ride some mounts as he had promised weeks earlier. The weather was awful and although Archer appeared in the paddock in an enormous coat in an attempt to keep warm, he spent much of the time dressed only in thin racing silks. By the end of the meeting he was so weak that he had to ask Martin Gurry, a Newmarket trainer, to accompany him home as he feared he would collapse on the way. The doctor appeared immediately Archer got home and lost no time in diagnosing that he had acute typhoid fever. After four days in a state of semi-delirium the twenty-nine-year-old genius recovered sufficently to shoot himself with the gun he had always kept in his bedroom. The conflict of his iron will and his sensitivity, the physical toll of wasting and the death of his wife had brought on depression and illness which finally overcame him. It was one of the greatest tragedies – and sensations – in racing history. Thousands of people, owners, trainers, his fellow jockeys and – more widely – his adoring public, were stunned by the news. In spite of his untimely death, Archer achieved a breakthrough for racing by becoming the first figure in the sport to be known to the public at large. Very few men have achieved his sort of legendary status and one can only speculate as to what heights he would have reached if he had lived longer.

Archer was unrivalled in his own lifetime in his number of wins – only Steve Donaghue, Sir Gordon Richards and Lester Piggott have approached his records. Yet surprisingly, for some of his contemporaries, Archer was not the most accomplished horseman of his time.

One of the most experienced of these, John Osborne, another jockey, said many years after Archer's death, 'There's been a lot of good jockeys. Jim Robinson was a good jockey and so was Fred Archer, but I am inclined to

The pistol with which Fred Archer shot himself.

think Fordham was the best of all; you never quite knew where you had him.' Archer himself would appear to have held George Fordham in similar respect and he was always the jockey he feared most. 'In one race George comes and taps me in the last stride on the post. I am determined not to have this happen again, and then in the next race he just gets home and I beat him a stride past the post; with his clucking and fiddling you never know what the old chap is up to.' Leopold de Rothschild once took the liberty of giving Danny Maher his opinion of jockeys in general, just after Maher had ridden a winner for him: 'With all due deference to you, Maher, the best jockey I have seen in my life – you included – is Fordham.' Maher's reply was politely non-committal: 'So I have always heard, sir.'

Fordham was considerably older than Archer and had been champion jockey on many occasions before the young star emerged. He only won the Derby once but he was a supreme horseman, a brilliant judge of pace and of a finish. He was the greatest exponent of 'the waiting game' which many jockeys rode through the nineteenth century, delaying their bid for victory to a very late stage, and a tactic which was fast disappearing by the beginning of the twentieth century. His style of explaining a victory was often as faltering as the way in which he won. He was famous for getting off a horse and saying to the owner and trainer: 'Well, don't you see, I just went up and – er – don't you know, I – er – just managed to win.' He rode well into middle-age, but gave up for some time when he took heavily to drink. His comeback was welcomed with an air of celebration, but throughout his career he scared the wits out of many trainers, owners and not least punters by his last-minute tactics. Despite his placid and self-effacing manner he was not prepared to suffer any speculation about his integrity and honesty as a jockey, whoever it came from. Captain Machell made the mistake of accusing Fordham of not trying when he was beaten on one of the Captain's horses – which Machell had backed despite Fordham's warnings that the horse would not win. Fordham never rode for him again.

Archer and Fordham were both competitive, professional and honest men who did an enormous amount to secure the jockeys' reputation. Another was

123

George Lambton, surrounded by the Stanley House stable lads.

Tom Cannon, for many people the most stylish jockey of his time. Someone once remarked that during a race he had time to look down to see how finely his boots were polished. When he retired from riding he took up training at Danebury in Hampshire. George Lambton maintained that he was better at training jockeys than horses, and certainly there is the evidence to support his argument, for as well as his owns sons, Mornington and Kempton (named after the course) Cannon trained Jack Watts, a totally impassive jockey, who achieved his greatest moments of fame riding Persimmon. According to Richard Marsh, Watts only just allowed himself a smile as Persimmon was being led in after the Derby.

As racing gained more popular appeal, some of the leading jockeys became public heroes and attracted numerous ardent admirers. It was once darkly rumoured around Newmarket that the redoubtable Duchess of Montrose had developed a passion for Archer. For his part, the only interest Archer appears to have shown in the match was when he reputedly asked Captain Machell whether he would become a Duke if he married the Duchess.

To qualify as a jockey was the major ambition of the stable lads, the

diminutive boys – often early teenagers – who populated all racing stables. Life in a stable around the turn of the twentieth century was still pretty rough. Lads' wages were almost non-existent and virtually all of them lived in dormitories above the stables of the horses they 'did for'. They had board and lodging but many hardly ever saw their homes and families, often having left at the age of ten or twelve. Any time off – of which there was not much – would normally be spent in a communal sitting-room on one corner of the yard. The stable lads may not have been paid much but at the same time training fees averaged about £2 per week. Apart from the small number of leading stables most trainers may not have had more than a dozen or twenty horses in their yards during any one season.

Captain Machell was an exception among the professionals in that he managed rather than trained people's horses. Over the forty years that he was based at Bedford Cottage in Newmarket, where he employed a succession of trainers, he enjoyed remarkable success both in gaining winners for his patrons and with his own gambling. Shortly after he set up in Newmarket he achieved the most sensational victory of his life when Hermit (which he managed) won the Derby for Harry Chaplin, but contrary to popular opinion the Captain did not, like Chaplin, win a fortune. He took his money off the horse when Hermit broke a blood vessel before the race.

Many people would have agreed with Lord Rossmore that Captain Machell was the most astute man of his day on the Turf. He could occasionally reveal a somewhat dry sense of humour, as when one of his owners sought his advice when his wife had just left him. The Captain dozed off from boredom while the long and unhappy story was being told only to wake up with the opinion: 'Do with her? Why put her in a selling race and see what she fetches.'

To most people, however, he seemed a cold fish and, as he himself admitted, blighted by suspicion. It led to his loss of George Fordham and a few years later caused him even more grief. For many years Fred Archer had been a close friend of the Captain's and often gave him little-known tips about the horses he was riding. Shortly before a race near the end of his life, Archer advised the Captain to back the horse he was riding, called Queen Bee. (Partly because Archer knew that his friend would have been backing him in recent races when he had not been winning, and was therefore anxious to help him cover his losses.) In the event Queen Bee was narrowly beaten, despite all Archer's efforts. The Captain, rather than trust his friend to have given him a special piece of information, preferred to believe a woman standing close to him in the crowd who announced that Archer had told *her* that he would not win. Deluding himself that Archer had lied to him the Captain ignored the

jockey when he saw him after the race. For poor Archer – usually far more concerned about his friends when he lost than about himself – it was a cruel blow and possibly a contributing factor to his tragic end a few days later. When Archer killed himself shortly afterwards Machell was left wondering whether his unkindness had influenced his friend's suicide, and for the rest of his life was haunted by the pained expression that had flickered across the young man's sickly face.

None of the jockeys who followed Archer, Fordham and Tom Cannon quite matched up to the class of the three masters. However, to suffer by comparison with their illustrious predecessors was vastly preferable for the jockeys than the revolution in riding created by James Forman Sloan in 1897. Tod Sloan, as he was universally known, was an American who introduced the style of riding with short stirrups. At first it was contemptuously dismissed and Tod was referred to as 'a monkey up a stick'. But when he returned to ride in England again in the autumn of 1898, on a retainer from Lord William Beresford, he could not be ignored. After one of the autumn meetings at Newmarket Fred Rickaby ventured the opinion to George Lambton that, 'If I were an owner I should not run a horse unless Sloan rode it.' After a time some of the jockeys decided it was better to try to join Sloan than lose to him. When Sammy Loates was asked to ride a difficult horse which Sloan had already ridden to victory he said, 'I shall pull up my stirrups and do Tod Sloan on the old brute.' Halfway through the race, not only was Loates most uncomfortable but the horse seemed to sense it too and gave up trying. With a shout of, 'Here's two for old England,' Loates relaxed into his old seat and whipped the horse up to win easily.

Tod Sloan proved to be his own worst enemy. As a jockey he was brilliant and seemed capable of bringing off the most unexpected successes on some horses. In 1899 Lord William Beresford's horses – ridden by Sloan – won sixty races and a total of £42,000, only three seasons after he had begun his career as an owner. But the little American was arrogant, hot-tempered and extremely contentious. His riding tactics often left a lot to be desired and he was a compulsive gambler. They were not characteristics likely to endear him to either his fellow jockeys or the racing authorities.

Among a number of complaints made to the Jockey Club was one from Morny Cannon – by this time among the most senior and respected jockeys – about Sloan's riding in a race at Doncaster. Only the influence of his patron, Lord William, saved Sloan on many occasions, but it seemed inevitable that the aggressive American would overstep the mark. He eventually did so in the Cambridgeshire of 1900. Riding a horse called Codoman, which he was

certain would win. Sloan set about laying bets for huge sums of money through his various cronies, weeks before the race. The only rival was a horse called Berrill. Sloan and his gang of friends tried every possible trick to either secure the ride on Berrill for a safe jockey or to stop the horse getting to the post – even going so far as to attempt to nobble him. But Berrill got to

Tod Sloan: 'the monkey up a stick', who introduced riding with short stirrups from America.

Newmarket safely and duly won the race with Sloan second. It was too much for Tod, and his subsequent abusive and threatening outburst against Thompson, Berrill's jockey, was too much for the Stewards of the Jockey Club, when they got to hear about it. At the end of the season Sloan was told

Above and below: Two styles of riding – with long and short stirrups.

bluntly that he need not bother to apply for a jockey's licence again, because it would not be forthcoming. Despite his premature departure, Sloan's contemporaries came to realize the benefits of his style of riding, which soon became widespread.

Amateurs or gentlemen were almost unheard of among the ranks of trainers, but in the early 1890s the dandyish figure of George Lambton appeared on the training scene. A younger brother of the Earl of Durham, Lambton had been a well-known character in the racing world for many years, notably as a gentleman rider. Unfortunately a fall at Sandown in 1892 ended his riding career.

Lambton was perpetually short of money and was a regular visitor to the well-known moneylender, Sam Lewis. Lewis was that rare commodity – an honest moneylender – and a friend to the racing fraternity, many of whom relied upon him for their betting cash. George Lambton was still in his twenties when, after a week of particularly heavy losses and in fear of his trustees, he made his first visit to Lewis's Cork Street office. 'When I was shown into his room I saw a little fat man with a bald head sitting at the desk smoking a big cigar. As I proceeded to explain who I was he said, "Never mind about that, I know all about you young man; you have been betting very high and have got no money. I have been expecting you here for some time. What can I do for you?"' Shortly afterwards, when Lambton's finances had gone from bad to worse, his family and trustees threatened to send him to Canada to allow time to straighten out his affairs and keep him off the Turf. Lewis got to hear of the plan, and saved his young client from exile by having him arrested as a debtor and only released when it was safe for him to stay in England.

A year after his fall at Sandown, Lambton was approached by Lord Stanley, son of the 15th Earl of Derby, and asked whether he would train for his father and himself. Lord Derby had recently inherited from the 14th Earl, who had had a lifelong dislike and suspicion of the Turf, and he and his son had decided to revive the family's previously prestigious racing fortunes. The offer was the answer to all Lambton's problems and after Lord Stanley inherited and became the 16th Earl the two men were to enjoy one of the most successful and important racing partnerships in history.

Years of watching horses and close friendship with most of the leading trainers, jockeys and owners had given Lambton considerable knowledge and experience which he put to good use. The re-emergence of the Derby family's racing enterprises was also well timed. As a result of the death of Squire Baird in 1893 Lambton was able to begin training at the vacant Bedford Lodge

Sam Lewis: money-lender, and friend of many a desperate punter.

The Earl of Derby and George Lambton: one of racing's most successful partnerships ever.

Stables, which he leased from Baird's executors. A more important death yet was that of Caroline, Duchess of Montrose. At the dispersal sale of her horses in 1894 Lambton purchased the yearling filly called Canterbury Pilgrim for his new exployers. A few years later they were able to buy the site of the Duchess's Sefton Stud where the new Stanley House stables were built. On completion they were the most modern and lavish training establishment in Newmarket.

Canterbury Pilgrim gave Lambton and the Derbys their first Classic by winning the Oaks in 1896. (The victory was not, however, greeted with universal celebration,as the horse in second place was the Prince of Wales's Thais. Although he did not complain officially, the Prince took the opportunity of telling Lambton that Canterbury Pilgrim's jockey, Fred Rickaby, had steered unnecessarily close to his horse). Far more important than her Classic win was Canterbury Pilgrim's career as a brood mare. When retired to stud at the Derby's seat in Lancashire, Knowsley Park, she was one of the three mares who founded all their future successes.

During the years of Edward VII's reign George Lambton and the Stanley House stables were a dominant influence in Newmarket. When the King died Lambton was fifty, but it was in the twenty-five years of George V's reign that he and Lord Derby's horses were to enjoy almost unrivalled success. By the time that Lambton died in 1945 he had outlived almost all of his Edwardian contemporaries and had known intimately most of the leading figures in racing for well over half a century. He had seen the role of the trainer develop from being a mixture of tradesman and personal servant to a skilled and often lucrative profession. Having himself been the first gentleman trainer he was to see increasing participation by upper-class young men. Not least, his memoir, *Men and Horses I Have Known* is the best contemporary account of the racing world of the Edwardian era.

ON THE COURSE

On the coaches at Royal Ascot.

By the end of the nineteenth century racecourses had become as important as meeting places for Society as they were for the sport. Whereas in the middle of the century racing crowds were still almost exclusively men – most of them mounted on their own hacks, as it was the only way to ensure a good view of the racing – by 1900 all the main courses had stands and Tattersall's and members' enclosures, the two being clearly separated. As today, the bookmakers took up position in Tattersall's, close to the rail dividing it from the members' enclosure, thus enabling members of society to wander over and place their bets.

Bookmakers, or the Ring as they were collectively known, had been under the auspices of Tattersall's since the middle of the nineteenth century. At that time the Jockey Club found themselves frustrated in many of their attempts to push through the general reforms and improvements in racing by having to spend most of their time settling betting disputes. Having announced that they would have nothing more to do with betting differences, they authorized the Tattersall's Committee to take over the job. In 1886 the Committee issued the *Rules of Betting*, of which the opening rule ran: 'Tattersall's Committee

have authority to settle all questions relating to bets, commissions for bets, and any matters arising either directly or indirectly out of wagers or gaming transactions on horse racing, to adjudicate on all cases of default, and at their discretion, to report defaulters to the Jockey Club. If a defaulter is a partnership or a limited company, all or any of the partners or agents and all or any of the shareholders, directors, officers or agents of the defaulting company may be reported to the Jockey Club.' The bookmakers were not the only people to be reorganized by the Jockey Club in their attempts to improve affairs on racecourses. The Clerks of the Courses, responsible for the administration of the day's racing – the entries for races and the duties of the various officials such as the Starter and Judge – were urged to make every effort to improve the efficiency in the organization of a meeting. One of the main problems was punctuality, summarily sorted out at York racecourse by the following public announcement: 'The Clerk of the Course at York will regulate his watch by the clock of York Cathedral, and will be fined 5s for every minute he is behind time in the bell not ringing for the respective races.'

The poor Clerks still, however, had to deal with a multitude of unexpected problems, mostly over the entries for races, as shown by the following letter sent to Miles L'Anson (Clerk of a number of the northern courses for many years) in 1906:

> As you are one of the main men at Thirsk races will you put our Tom's chestnut gelding into the thirsk races to run which I am willing to pay for if he is tret as he should be tret in what he has to carry seeing as how he has only run at two flaps which I mention to you private and which our tom will ride him at thirsk if you don't give him overmuch wait. He is not quite thoroughbred but a blood sort and I would be willing to sell if you would find me a customer and make you a present as well. Perhaps you will borrow the things for Tom to ride in on the course as we haven't any except Tom has some hunting boots which will mebbe do. The horse can be seen here any day you come so no more at present.
>
> PS. John Osborne said I'd be able to train him at home better than he would so you'll see for yourself but I'll pay at the time as anythink might happen between now and Thirsk races which I attends reggler and has done for years.
> PS. Don't overdo him with wait and I supposes there'll be nothink to pay to come in this year seeing as how I'm fraternising the meeting.

Another from an irate Yorkshire trainer to Mr L'Anson ran as follows:

> I've got a bill for our horse being entered at Ripon and Pontrefract but it never ran having died previous with a stoppage in the bools. No man pays nothink

in no way to no one for a dead horse and I am put about at getting this blue paper from your London solicitor men. No true bred sportsman would have done such a trick. I'm willing to send you a ham but I pays nothink to no one in London and have sent no back answer.

The official with probably the most difficult task on the racecourse was the Starter. Before the starting gate was introduced towards the turn of the century – thereby providing a barrier in front of the horses and jockeys – he had only his personal authority and voice to try and impose order on proceedings. When crafty jockeys came up against inexperienced starters the result was havoc. The Starter at Northallerton racecourse resorted to taking one of the stewards of the course to help enforce discipline at the start. It was not, however, always the jockey's fault. One Starter at Goodwood had such a bad speech impediment that when he got over-excited the jockeys could not distinguish whether he was saying, 'Go!' or 'No!' In the end the success of the Jockey Club in imposing the threat of suspension or even warning-off on jockeys who misbehaved at the start, combined with a closer checking of the men appointed as Starters brought considerable improvements. And by 1905 the starting gate was compulsory on all courses.

Hand-in-hand with the more efficient organization of a day's racing went the scrutiny of those who attended, made possible by the charging of entrance-money and regular attendance by the police at racecourses. One contemporary summed up the changes when he wrote:

> Perhaps racing crowds are more law-abiding and peaceful than they were, perhaps it is only that the supervision is now much more complete, and that the supervisors are many more in number and better acquainted with those who bring racing into disrepute. It certainly costs much more to staff a race meeting in these days than it used to do at one time to run the whole fixture, stakes included; but the end has been attained, and it is economy in the long run now that all meetings are gate-money fixtures. It was the passing of the days of free admission which made this increase in staff necessary. And it was when gate-money meetings commenced that stakes were increased and crowds were placed under some measure of control. Incidentally it was then that some protection was given from sharps and welshers, and some provision was made for the comfort of the increasing racing public, for them to be able to see the whole of the races and to be able to move about both in the paddock and in the betting ring.

For the racing public, in particular the members of fashionable society, the most important meeting of the year was the week of Royal Ascot. As the period progressed so the parades at the royal meeting became more lavish. It

was the pinnacle of the London Season when, for four days, Society went on glorious public display. At the same time the meeting offered then, as it does now, more quality races than any other in the year. By the turn of the century as many as 150 race specials left Waterloo and Paddington stations during the royal meeting. In *Royal Ascot*, the authors, Cawthorne and Herod, describe the effect on London in early June:

> In the beginning of June a stranger to London would be amazed at the outward and visible signs of the Ascot stir in Society. Should he visit Waterloo or Paddington stations he will see innumerable piles of luggage, watched over by footmen, valets and servants, while stable hands are attending to horses and carriages, all consigned to Ascot or the surrounding country: if he pass down Bond Street, the long line of carriages that wait opposite Ashton's will appraise him that there the vouchers for the Royal Enclosure are exchanged and entrance tickets to the Grand Stand can be obtained.

Alice Keppel (centre), with her husband George and daughter Violet at Royal Ascot.

Even though Ascot was well equipped with stands by the turn of the century, carriages lined up on the opposite side of the course were always a great feature. Even as early as the 1870s, when there was a particularly large crowd there were over 180 coaches along the course. Naturally enough the exclusive 'Four-in-Hand' and 'Carriage' Clubs had their own enclosures, while more mortal drivers had to line up behind or further along the course. And as important as the horses were the clothes, for it was the Edwardians who initiated Ascot fashions and gave them their heyday during the reign of Edward VII. Lady Randolph Churchill remembers once wearing her wedding dress of white satin and point lace on Ascot Gold Cup day and although some of the fashions had changed by the end of the period, a description in *Royal Ascot* of the array for one year in the 1880s shows the absorbing interest and detail with which people were scrutinized:

> The Princess of Wales wore amber satin and black lace, with a bonnet to match. The handsome Duchess Ossima in a *manteau de cour* of brown satin striped gauze over yellow silk, attracted general admiration, as did the beautiful Lady Mary Dawson in pale primrose muslin (flounced), the Countess of March in bright yellow satin, and the fascinating Madame Becheve in dark blue velvet, over which was worn a pearl white *poult de soie polonaise*, without sleeves, the petticoat of which was trimmed with rich *point d'Alencon . . .* The Marchioness of Westminster was easily recognizable by her rich Indian mantle of claret and gold, the hew half shawls, or *point avere*, coming greatly into vogue. An attractive group on the rustic seat, below the Royal Saloon, included the Duchess of Manchester in pink silk, Lady Royston, and her sister Lady Feodorowna Wellesley in silver Grey with hats to correspond, but with contrasting streamers of violet and cerise velvet.

The fashions were not the only attraction for the ladies. Margot Asquith remembers meeting the Prince of Wales for the first time in her life at the paddock at Ascot. The meeting proved most productive:

> He asked me if I would back my fancy for the Wokingham Stakes and have a little bet with him on the race. We walked down to the rails and watched the horses gallop past. One of them went down in great form; I verified him by his colours and found that he was called Wokingham. I told the Prince that he was a sure winner; but out of so many entries no one was more surprised than I was when my horse came romping in. I was given a gold cigarette case and went home much pleased.

Margot Asquith was not the only lady to meet the Prince of Wales for the first time on a racecourse. In 1898 he was at Sandown and met the Hon Mrs

A touch of the Raj at Royal Ascot.

George Keppel who was to have such an influence on the remaining years of his life.

Not all of the Prince's encounters on the racecourse were as enjoyable as the one with Alice Keppel. In 1897, after Persimmon had won the Ascot Gold Cup, he was approached in the Royal Box by Lord Marcus Beresford. Lord Marcus was hoping to effect a reconciliation between the Prince and his younger brother, Lord Charles. But as the Prince revealed in a letter to Daisy Warwick, who had been the cause of the rift, he did not enjoy the encounter. Daisy had in fact been with the Prince to watch the race, but fortunately had left straight afterwards. Later the Prince of Wales wrote:

I lose no time in writing to tell you of an episode which occurred today after you left – wh. was unpleasant & unexpected – but I hope my darling you will agree that I could not have acted otherwise, as my loyalty to you, is I hope, a thing that you will never think of doubting! Shortly before leaving Ascot today, Marcus B. came to me, & said he had a gt. favour to ask me – so I answered at once I should be delighted to grant it. He then became much affected & actually cried & said might he bring his brother C. up to me to offer his congratulations on 'Persimmon's' success. I had no alternative but to say yes. He came up with his hat off & would not put it on till I told him, & shook hands. We talked a little about racing, then I turned and we parted. What struck me more than anything was his humble attitude & manners!

For many of the ladies the clothes and the gossip were the serious business of a day's racing and they were content to watch the succession of races with little or no knowledge of what was going on. One young lady who had seen four jockeys, Archer, Watts, Barrett and Wood disappear into the Stewards' Room, summoned for disobedience at the post, remarked blithely to her companion, 'How very nice of the Duke of Beaufort to ask those jockeys to lunch after winning the Cup!' Another who rather energetically decided to walk out onto the course to watch the start of a race, returned to tell a friend that the race in progress was a handicap. When corrected and told that in fact it was a weight-for-age she persisted in her opinion: 'Oh no, I am sure it is a handicap. Mr Coventry started them one by one and that's a handicap isn't it?' The ladies were not always very popular with the experts such as General Owen Williams who, on trying to get to the edge of the paddock to watch one of his two-year-olds being saddled at Ascot found his path blocked by a woman with a large red parasol. At the same time the brilliant shade of the parasol made one of the horses rear and the alarmed lady leapt back, stabbing the poor general in the cheek with the tip of her parasol and crying indignantly: 'It's perfectly *scandalous* that horses should be allowed in here.'

As befitting at an occasion of such social importance, the luncheon interval at Royal Ascot was one of the highlights of the day. Here, and at other main meetings, a period was specifically set aside for what was rarely the al fresco racing picnic as we know it today. In the Grand Stand in the Royal Enclosure at Ascot there were, as well as the boxes, a series of private luncheon rooms and a large dining hall, both served by the staff of Mr Browning, the exclusive on-course caterer. (Shortly before the turn of the century one race-goer observed that Mr Browning had achieved a notable breakthrough in the catering on racecourses by making it possible to buy a decent, fresh lobster at Ascot.) To ensure that the dining hall did not become like a conservatory the glass roof of the surrounding balcony was kept constantly cool by being covered by flowing water.

Both at Ascot and the other main courses the luncheon interval was the opportunity for eating and socializing – two important priorities. Those who did not go to the stands consumed the contents of enormous hampers on their carriages or, at Goodwood for instance, in the shade of the trees behind the main stand known as the Luncheon Grove.

If Royal Ascot was the highspot of Society's Season, Derby Day a few weeks earlier was the greatest national carnival of the year. Every year tens of thousands of people poured onto Epsom Downs, on foot, on horseback, by carriage or by train. The Prince of Wales only missed it if he was in court mourning and the House of Commons went into recess for the day. Lord Brampton, a famous judge, always ensured that his cases on Derby Day were adjourned in time for him to get away to Epsom. His love of racing was well-known: on one occasion the clerk of the court ordered a man to stop rustling a newspaper. Leaning over, the judge spied that it was a copy of *The Sporting Life* ('*The Pink 'Un*') and asked whether he could borrow it during the luncheon interval.

The traffic to and from Epsom on Derby Day was non-stop, by train and road and for twenty-four hours the small suburban town was the scene of much high-spirited chaos. Even Mr Gladstone, certainly not a racing enthusiast,

Chevalier Ginistrelli, hero of the Epsom crowd, with his formidable wife.

accepted the inconvenience caused by Derby Day. One year he was expecting the Archbishop of Canterbury and his wife to dinner but they failed to appear. Eventually Gladstone decided that the party could wait no longer and moved towards the dining-room, remarking absent-mindedly: 'We must not forget that it is Derby Day. His Grace has evidently been delayed by the congested traffic on his way back from Epsom.'

Possibly infected by the holiday atmosphere of the day, the crowd at Epsom was almost unfailingly enthusiastic and generous, and never more so than in 1908 when the Derby was won by the eccentric Chevalier Odorato Ginistrelli. The diminutive Chevalier bred a few horses which he trained himself in a most unorthodox manner at Newmarket. He was regarded with affectionate amusement by most of the racing fraternity. Towards the end of the 1880s the Chevalier had enjoyed some success with a filly called Signorina and was most upset when, after her retirement to stud, she proved to be barren for the first ten years. .

Eventually, in 1904, she produced her first foal. (The sire was a stallion of no consequence called Chaleureux. His capabilities, or lack of them, hardly interested the Chevalier who had sent Signorina to the stallion because he was convinced they were in love with one another.) The mutual affection obviously did the trick and the love-child was named Signorinetta. With no foundation for his theory, her adoring owner became convinced that she would win the Derby and began preparing her for the great race in his individual hand-to-mouth style. As luck would have it, the field for the Derby of 1908 was rather weak and Signorinetta won at the sensational odds of 100 to 1. Recognizing a sportsman, the disbelieving crowd for once swallowed their nationalist prejudices and gave the delighted little Italian a hero's welcome as he led in his horse. As it turned out, the Derby was only half the story. Two days later Signorinetta went out again at Epsom and won the Oaks. This time Edward VII was as fascinated as the crowd. Having sent for the Chevalier, the King led him to the front of the Royal Box to acknowledge the cheers from below.

For many people the actual racing was of little or no consequence. There was certainly much else to see: gypsies, clowns, conjurers and other entertainers. In 1899, the year Flying Fox won the Derby on his way to the Triple Crown, one well-known bookmaker named Palmer attempted to draw custom by displaying a live, but terrified fox, chained to his stand. But if the downs were covered with holiday-makers and an extraordinary mixture of humanity, the enclosure and grandstand contained the serious race-goers and members of society. There the clothes were as immaculate as they would

Epsom town centre on Derby Day.

An accident on the way to the Derby.

be later for Ascot and morning dress was *de rigeur* for men. Certainly nobody but the Duke of Devonshire could have got away with his constant untidiness and after he had been seen for many years in the same old and deteriorating hat, a number of ladies decided to club together and buy him a new one.

One of the Prince of Wales's obsessions throughout his life was correct dress. As far as he was concerned if you could not wear medals or decorations properly you did not deserve them. His intolerance extended to dress on the racecourse and Lord Rossmore incurred the royal wrath for appearing at the Derby in a bowler hat instead of the statutory silk top hat. 'Well, Rossmore, have you come r-r-r-ratting,' the Prince enquired caustically. When a foreign diplomat asked whether it was permissible for him to go racing when his Court was in mourning he was firmly told that he could not go to the Derby – where he would need to wear a top hat – but he could attend Newmarket where a bowler was acceptable. Sir John Astley was one of the very few people to get away with a joke on the subject. The Prince caught sight of the Mate in the Royal Enclosure at Ascot in a short-tailed coat and told him that he should come properly dressed. The next day the Mate turned up and presented himself to the Prince wearing the same coat, but with two large buttons sewn on the back where they would be on a full tail-coat. Fortunately His Royal Highness was amused.

Derby Day and Royal Ascot were the racing highlights of the summer season, the end of which was marked by the week at Goodwood in July. Goodwood had been laid out towards the beginning of the century by Lord George Bentinck for the 5th Duke of Richmond, whose descendants maintained the family's racing interests. Its wonderful setting gave Goodwood an exclusive atmosphere, as befitted a race meeting on the private land of a great aristocrat, but there was also an air of relaxation which reflected that members of society were taking a rest after the hectic summer weeks. Picnics were normally the order of the day for luncheon, but few people proved as resourceful as Colonel North – known as 'The Nitrate King' as he had gone to Chile without a penny and made himself a millionaire through nitrates – who was well-known for his love of food. Disturbed during his lunch by an unexpected downpour of rain, he went out onto the downs side of the course and persuaded one of the gypsies to sell him his tent which he then had erected under the trees to enable him to finish his lunch in peace and dry conditions.

In contrast to the ducal grandeur of Goodwood, Doncaster, the scene of the most important autumn meeting – for the St Leger – was the property of the Doncaster Town Council. The Town Moor course, as it is known, lies on the outskirts of Doncaster and is considerably older than Goodwood. The

Gypsies on Epsom Downs.

A religious meeting attracts a crowd.

A wet Epsom.

Dreaming of the winner, or sleeping it off.

St Leger was first run in 1778. The Race Committee was almost invariably composed of prominent Doncaster burghers, including the mayor.

One factor which brought all levels of race-goers together was betting. A major difference between racing then and in later years was the level of betting by owners of racehorses, a situation partly accounted for by the Duke of Portland when he explained that for much of the period only the Classics and a few other races were worth over £1,000 and it was impossible to cover racing expenses by stakes won. Not many owners hoped to finance their racing expenses by betting like Sir George Chetwynd, but there were very few who did not back their own horses regularly and often heavily.

The Duke of Hamilton was one of the best-known heavy gamblers and in *Old Pink 'Un Days*, J. B. Booth recalls one of the Duke's more spectacular punts. Approaching one of his favourite bookies called Saffrey, he asked what price his horse.

> 'Seven to one, your Grace', replied Saffrey.
> 'Seven thousand to one Saffrey – pounds not francs.'
> 'Right your Grace!'
> 'Twice, Saffrey.'
> 'Right your Grace!'
> 'Three times Saffrey.'
> 'I'll make it 6 to 1 this time your Grace. Shall we make it £20,000 to £3,000?'
> 'Right Saffrey.'

Up until the arrival of the Prince of Wales, the Duke of Hamilton was Richard Marsh's principle owner. Poor Marsh recalls being made to 'flush with anxiety by the way his Grace would bring his big guns to bear on the bookmakers.' A huge, bluff man who spent almost as much time upon his yacht *Thistle* as he did on dry land, his Grace was Scotland's premier Duke and had no illusions about the nobility of his descent which, as far as he was concerned, compared favourably with any member of the Royal Family. On one occasion at Egerton he threw Marsh into a frenzy by being half an hour late when due to go round evening stables with the Prince of Wales.

> 'Your Grace is half an hour late. The Prince has been waiting for you on the lawn.'
> 'Oh, that's all right, Marsh. Don't worry. I thought I would look in at the sale paddocks and I bought a yearling. Anyway, take me into the house and give me a whiskey-and-soda first.'

Though they often bet spectacularly, despite their extensive knowledge of horses and their form, there were very few owners who ever made any money

Doncaster Race Committee: all members of the Town Council and headed by the Mayor.

out of their betting. Lord Alington, undoubtedly one of the shrewdest men on the Turf, once confided to John Corlett, editor of *The Sporting Times*, that he had had nineteen bets on the Cesarewitch and they had all lost. And the maligned Lord Stamford complained, 'I have lost a quarter of a million of money on the Turf and yet I am called a sharp.'

One of the few who did make any money was Jack Hammond, who began life as a stable lad working for Captain Machell. He could hardly have had a better tutor, for as well as being an astute judge of a horse, Machell was successful enough through his own gambling to buy back his old family home. Hammond regularly bet small amounts on favourites but reserved his really big punts for outsiders which he fancied. His judgement normally paid off. In 1882 Dutch Oven, owned by Lord Falmouth and ridden by Fred Archer, won the Yorkshire Oaks and like many others Hammond backed her at 8 to 1 to win the St Leger when she would be up against Geheimniss, who had won the Oaks. But in between times Dutch Oven ran very poorly in another race, with the result that she went to 66 to 1 for the St Leger and Geheimniss became a hot favourite. Archer even tried to persuade Lord Falmouth to allow him to swop horses to Geheimniss, but to no avail. While

most people were getting off Dutch Oven as fast as they could Hammond stood by his judgement and must have been very satisfied when she came in the winner. His greatest coup was in 1884, the year his horse St Gatien dead-heated with Harvester for the Derby. Hammond reserved his big bets for the autumn double, the Cesarewitch and the Cambridgeshire. Having won £90,000 on St Gatien on the first race, a fortnight later he won £75,000 when Florence won the second. Both St Gatien's and Florence's origins were as humble as Jack Hammond's: St Gatien's sire had pulled a cab while Florence's dam had pulled a farmer's cart. This notwithstanding, Jack left £100,000 from his betting when he died.

The appetite for gambling and, more particularly, the control of the betting ring led to the gradual disappearance of 'welshers'. Welshers, bookies who took your money but were nowhere to be found if your horse won, were without question the most hated of all racecourse crooks. If caught they were usually subjected to a terrible vengeance by an enraged racing crowd. The treatment differed from course to course: at Catterick they were tarred and feathered, while at any course close to a river they were stripped naked and thrown into the water. More than one welsher was done to death. In their place came the honest bookmakers, who combined shrewdness with wit and were among the best-known of all racing figures. Richard (Dick) Dunn was one of these so-called 'Leviathans of the Ring'. By the time he died – a very rich man – in 1905, Dick had become something of an institution, as described by one contemporary writer:

> Years ago he was dubbed the Lord Chesterfield, but a better name would be the Tallyrand, of the Ring. A list of his smart sayings would choke up the British Museum, and I never saw him nonplussed but once, and that was when a railway guard wanted two points over the odds. Well do I remember the first wager I had with Dick. 'Take care of your ticket, sir' he chaunted in his most dulcet tones, 'or some evil-doer will relieve you of it.' The last time the chaunt was in the minor key. 'Here! Take your bloomin' custom somewhere else: I'm tired of payin' you!' He who saw D. D. in the Ring for the first time would probably marvel at the beauty and sparkle of his diamonds. Next he would admire the neat attire of the bookmaker and 'Sobersides' his clerk. But what would strike the observer most is the *voice* of the man . . . It is certain that his voice is the most powerful as well as the most tuneful I have ever heard . . . Had the subject of my notice cared to enter the political arena, he would have been Prime Minister long before this . . . As it is, Dick probably makes the biggest ready-money book in the Ring, has one of the largest mansions in London, and the best tailor, and, moreover, pays him. He has a most genial disposition and the readiest of wits. He has diamonds which would make a

duchess turn pale with envy . . . He has a fine stud of horses and a bowing acquaintance with two-thirds of the inhabitants of the United Kingdom. He has an income which far exceeds that of the Lord Chancellor. And the gout has got him.

For many years Dunn's stentorian voice could be heard resounding round most of the courses in England. His favourite was Hurst Park, close to his home and where the London tradesmen would go for a Saturday afternoon off. He called them 'my little Saturday afternoon punters' and always gave them good odds for their bets of a few shillings. A different clientèle attended Stockbridge races, particularly for the annual meeting of the Bibury Club when most of the races were for amateur riders. On one occasion when a

Dick Dunn: Leviathan of the betting ring.

young aristocrat was winning by a long way, but continually looking round to ensure he was safe, Dunn's voice was heard booming good-naturedly:'It's all right; hounds have gone the other way m'lord.' He often gave the appearance of being fierce with some of the more reckless and inexperienced gamblers, as at Goodwood when he once offered 50 to 1 to a desperate looking individual for a combination in the second and third races. When the first horse won the overjoyed punter danced up to the bookie's stand shouting, 'It's won – it's won!' before collapsing in a faint from excitement. When Sobersides, Dunn's clerk enquired nervously, 'Shall I fetch him some brandy gov'nor?' Dunn, quite unmoved replied, 'Let the perisher be an' go an' get a wreath!' By and large Dunn was unfailingly generous-hearted and by the time he died had given thousands of pounds to various charities.

Fortunately for him, Dunn was not the unlucky bookmaker who had to pay out when Lord Randolph Churchill won a considerable amount of money on the Oaks as the result of a dream. He had dreamt that a winning number appeared on the board and, trusting to providence, laid a large bet because the number turned out to be the only high one on the card and the horse an outsider. Such rashness was uncharacteristic of Lord Randolph who took up racing in 1887 when he retired from the Government. He began in partnership with Lord Dunraven and was soon acknowledged to be a shrewd judge of form. It was reported that on the morning of a big meeting, he would sit for hours pencilling upon the card by the aid of *Ruff's Guide*, calculations which very often led to conclusions that were right. When he embarked on his career as an owner he remarked with some arrogance to Sir Frederick Johnstone, who warned him that he was not rich enough to race on the scale he was buying yearlings, 'Nearly all you people who go racing are fools, and no really clever man has ever taken it up seriously, but now that I have done so I shall succeed.' It must have come as a blow to his pride when, not long afterwards, he approached his jockey, Fred Rickaby, who was coming in on one of Lord Randolph's winners and asked him how the horse had run. Rickaby, not recognizing him, and mistaking him for a tout, replied abusively: 'What the hell is it to do with you!' and it was only through the intervention of the trainer that Rickaby was not sacked there and then.

By the turn of the century the plungers of the nineteenth century who regularly bet in thousands were disappearing. So too were the bookies prepared to make a really big or, at times outrageously adventurous, book. One nearly ruined himself when he laid £20,000 to an owner's coat, waistcoat and hat and the horse was only just beaten. Besides those men who were regular or well-known defaulters, there was a certain cameraderie between

bookmakers and betters, as shown by the story of the bookie who visited a racing peer who owed him a considerable amount of money. 'I'll give you a good lunch, as much wine as you can drink and as many pheasants as you can carry home, but I *can't give you any money* for the simple reason I haven't got any.' The bookie went away resigned to his losses.

The runners approach . . .

and, time to celebrate.

THE LADIES

The height of fashion: ladies at Goodwood.

Betting was something that the ladies were able to enjoy and, especially if they were not really interested in the horses, it brought a note of excitement to a day's racing. For many of them it was a question of modest sums of pin-money — although they were never above trying on a bit of guile. One attractive young peeress approached George Drake, one of the best-known bookmakers, at York and asked innocently, 'If I have a fiver on the favourite at 6 to 4, how much shall I win if it very nearly wins and comes in second?' As there were only three horses in the race Drake had no hesitation in replying, 'I'll make you a present of the horse, madam.'

One lady who enjoyed betting and was usually extremely successful, was the formidable Louise, Duchess of Manchester. George Lambton once got a severe dressing down because he forgot to put on a bet for the Duchess and

the horse won at 33 to 1. Lord Rossmore learnt to his cost that it was better to be with the Duchess than against her where horses were concerned. They were both staying with Reuben Sassoon for Lewes races where Rossmore had a particularly good two-year-old running. Unfortunately Sassoon drove so recklessly on the way to the races that the Duchess – fearing the carriage would tip over – demanded that they stop and that the horses walk the rest of the way. As a result they arrived too late for Rossmore to bet on his horse which won easily. Complaining testily to the Duchess that she had deprived him of a winner, she replied with gusto, 'Well, I am very glad that it didn't win as you never told *me* anything about it!'

The Duchess never forgave Sir William Gordon Cumming after he came up to her at Ascot and asked, 'When is Harty-Tarty going to make an honest woman of you?' No one was more delighted than the Duchess by his downfall after Tranby Croft. Sir William had been referring to her liaison with the Marquess of Hartington which lasted for thirty years. As a young woman, the Duchess's beauty was renowned, to the extent that one of her contemporaries wrote in old age, 'No one knows how beautiful a woman can be who did not see the Duchess of Manchester when she was thirty.' Shortly after her marriage to the Duke of Manchester she realized that there was nothing more to her husband than his looks, wealth and titles. As he preferred the affections of an East End music-hall actress called Bessie Bellwood, she happily embarked on her affair with Hartington. The Duchess had all the ambition that Hartington could not be bothered to muster, and she alternately drove and encouraged him through his political career. It is quite certain that she was far more disappointed than he ever was that Hartington did not become Prime Minister; if he had done so it would have been in no small part due to her. Confident of her position, Louise was able to ignore his occasional lapses, in particular his affection for the notorious Catherine Walters – known as 'Skittles' – the most renowned courtesan of her day. She was unable, however, to prevent his heir from continuing to pay the £2,000 per annum which Hartington had given to Skittles at the end of their liaison as a token of his affection. Throughout the thirty years the Duchess and Hartington conducted themselves in public with faultless formality, only using each other's titles. They only slipped once: staying at Welbeck with the Duke of Portland, Louise was writing letters and Portland's mother overheard her ask Hartington, who was standing close by, 'Harty darling, stand me a stamp.'

Eventually they were married – in absolute privacy in London – in 1892, the year Louise's reprobate first husband died and the year after Hartington had become Duke of Devonshire. As a result of her unique distinction Louise

The Double Duchess.

was forever after known as 'the Double Duchess'. It became a tradition for her to entertain Princess Alexandra at Devonshire House while the Prince was entertaining the Jockey Club at his Derby Day dinner, which he would leave with Devonshire to join his wife. Towards the end of her life cards and racing were the Duchess's favourite pastime. She died in 1911 after suffering a heart attack while at Sandown, from which she never recovered.

E.F. Benson wrote about Louise that, 'there was something of the unswerving relentlessness of a steam-roller about her' . . . and certainly she was not worth upsetting, as many people discovered to their cost. Lady Fingall did so, although her affront was caused quite unconsciously. One day at Newmarket she absent-mindedly sat down on a bench below the Jockey Club stand, not knowing that it was reserved for the exclusive use of the Prince of Wales and those ladies with whom he wished to chat. The Duchess was quick to point out her error – and equally quick to anger when the Prince himself arrived on the scene and, not only invited Lady Fingall to remain where she was, but sat down beside her. A few months later Lady Fingall's name was conspicuously absent from the list of invitations for the Duchess's famous Fancy-dress Ball in 1897.

Even for someone as grand as the Duchess, it seemed that pride came before the fall. At the coronation of King Edward VII, she not only lost her dignity

but appears to have overrated her importance. As the royal party left Westminster Abbey the haughty lady was quick to leave her seat and follow in their path, only to find the way barred by Grenadier Guards, with clear instructions to allow a proper time to elapse between the departure of the various royalties, and anyone else. Incensed at such treatment, the Duchess attempted to pass but, as Sir Almeric Fitzroy recorded in his memoirs:

> She fell heavily forward and rolled over on her back at the feet of Sir Michael Hicks-Beach, who was just leaving his stall; her coronet fell off and struck the stalls at some distance from the spot. The Chancellor of the Exchequer was too paralysed by the suddenness of the apparition to offer any assistance; but willing hands, directed by the indefatigable Soveral, at last restored the illustrious lady to her legs. Mrs Asquith secured her coronet and placed it on her head, and after some little attention to her ruffled hair she was permitted to proceed, not apparently much the worse for the accident.

The Duchess of Devonshire's chief rival as the greatest hostess of the period was Theresa, Marchioness of Londonderry, who was equally fond of racing and reckoned by George Lambton to be more knowledgeable about horses than most of the men he knew. The imposing Marchioness casually referred to the Londonderry family tiara – famed for the size of its jewels – as the family fender. Unfortunately, as with the Duchess of Devonshire, it caused

The Marchioness of Londonderry – weighed down by the 'family fender', as well as other Londonderry jewels.

her the worst moment of her life at Edward VII's Coronation, when she dropped the priceless heirloom into the lavatory-pan in the Peeresses room at Westminster Abbey.

If most of the ladies enjoyed gambling, by and large they managed to do so with a degree of restraint. Very few of them indulged quite so recklessly or disastrously as Jessica Sykes, whose husband, Sir Tatton Sykes, owned one of the best-known studs in England. Jessica was a cousin of the Duke of Portland, but as different in temperament from the bland Duke as she was from her husband. Wilful, impetuous and over-sexed, she proved quite beyond the control of the introvert, fastidious Sir Tatton.

The stud at Sledmere, the family seat in Yorkshire, had become famous in the middle of the nineteenth century when owned by Sir Tatton's father – also Sir Tatton. The reputation was for the quantity, rather than the quality of the horses; there were hundreds, very few of which old Sir Tatton ever got round to naming. After his death in 1863 his son realized that a new start was necessary to improve the stud and sold off all except one of his father's horses. Young Sir Tatton was not interested in racing his horses himself but around the turn of the century his new stud was very profitable. Probably the best horse he bred was Doncaster, who won the Derby in 1873 and was the foundation of the Duke of Westminster's stud at Eaton.

During the first few years of her marriage Jessica managed to find some sort of fulfilment in charitable works in Yorkshire and London. Unfortunately the commitment did not last long and she was soon dangerously frustrated with life. At first she turned to Roman Catholicism but it proved only a temporary refuge. Even before she embraced the faith her wildness was becoming increasingly well known and talked about in London. She became known as 'Lady Satin Tights'. Spending much of her time – not to mention her husband's money – on drinking and gambling, by the 1890s Jessica was heading for disaster. The final blow came when Jack Gorst, with whom she had been carrying on a passionate affair, suddenly ditched her. The depth to which she had sunk was described by her great-grandson, Christopher Sykes, in *The Visitors' Book*: 'By the mid-1890s Jessica's drinking had become so bad that her maid had resorted to hiding her scent lest she take to drinking it again. Sometimes, when Jesscia was in a particularly bad state, she took to hiding her stays so that she could not go out and disgrace herself while haunting the bookmakers' shops in Henrietta Street'.

By the end of 1896 Sir Tatton was desperate. In an attempt to stem the ever mounting tide of Jessica's debts he took the unprecedented step of putting

Jessica Sykes: better at riding horses than backing them.

an announcement in *The Times*. Not surprisingly, it caused a major sensation.

> I, Sir Tatton Sykes, Baronet of Sledmere in the county of York, and 46 Grosvenor Street in the county of London, hereby give notice that I will NOT BE RESPONSIBLE for any DEBTS or ENGAGEMENTS which my wife LADY JESSICA CHRISTINA SYKES may contract, whether purporting to be on my behalf or by my authority or otherwise.

The announcement could not have had a worse effect. Within days Jessica's creditors were crowding in for payment. It was not long before a money lender, from whom Jessica had borrowed over £10,000 at huge rates of interest, took out a court action against both Jessica and Sir Tatton to secure his money. The sum had been gained by Jessica with promissory notes which she asserted were signed by Sir Tatton. But he denied this and in court the jury decided that the signatures were indeed forgeries. The case was widely publicized and closely followed by both members of society and the general public – many of the former with some trepidation, the latter with widespread glee at yet another example of the rich upper classes making themselves a public laughing-stock.

The court case brought a forcible end to Jessica's gambling and extravagance. For the rest of her life she concentrated on writing which had long been one of her passions. She died in 1912, still only in middle age, but her health had been seriously impaired by years of heavy drinking. As for Sir Tatton, he had returned to Sledmere totally humiliated only to be beset by another disaster a few years later when the great house was almost completely destroyed by a fire in 1911. He only outlived his wife by one year and died in a London hotel in 1913.

The excesses and final demise of Jessica Sykes were a stern warning to her contemporaries about both the follies of uncontrolled gambling and the dangers of getting into the clutches of avaricious and extortionate money lenders. It was a widely accepted practice for many people to be virtually dependent on money lenders for their ready cash, especially young men who had not come into their inheritance or were tightly controlled by trustees. More acres of private estates were sold during the period to pay off enormous debts run up with creditors than for any other single reason.

The ladies may have been allowed to gamble, but behaviour like that of Jessica Sykes was totally unacceptable. There was also a strong convention against their owning racehorses. Of the few who did so, running their horses under assumed names, the most intrepid and resourceful was Caroline, Duchess of Montrose, who ran her horses under the name of 'Mr Manton'. During her lifetime the Duchess had three husbands, but when aged seventy she was heard to say, 'I never allow any man to come into my bedroom except Mr Alec Taylor, and he is always welcome.' Alec Taylor was her trainer and, despite his popularity with his patron, had no illusions about the Duchess's tempestuousness if her horses did not win. After one win when she congratulated him enthusiastically saying, 'What a good trainer you are!' Taylor replied philosophically, 'Yes, when I win.' One of her many jockeys, Harry Huxtable, showed himself to be equally quick-witted when the Duchess lambasted him for failing to win a race, 'I thought I told you to come away and win when you got to the distance.' Undismayed Huxtable replied, 'I am sorry Your Grace, but I should have had to come along without the horse.'

The Duke of Montrose died in 1874 and Caroline outlived him by twenty years, continuing to use her title. In 1876 she married William Stirling Crawfurd who was already a successful owner. In 1878 his horse, Sefton, won the Derby. In 1881 another of his horses, Thebias, won the One Thousand Guineas and the Oaks, but the next year caused a sensation at the Newmarket autumn meeting. Crawfurd won the Cesarewitch with Corrie Roy and

Thebias was made a hot favourite to complete the autumn double by winning the Cambridgeshire a few days later. Shortly before the race, however, the Duchess withdrew Thebias, to the fury of the crowd. Deprived of what they hoped would be a certain double they booed loudly next time she appeared at the races. But the formidable Duchess was not one to be put off by a few angry punters, or by the offensive ditty which appeared in one of the sporting papers about her and her husband 'Craw':

> Isn't Craw a lucky boy?
> With Carrie Red and Corrie Roy
> With Corrie Roy and Carrie Red,
> One for the course and one for the bed.

The Duchess was dictatorial in the management of her horses, trainers and jockeys alike. Her manner was complimented by her ample figure, the

Alec Taylor (left): the Duchess of Montrose's trainer, and the only man allowed into her bedroom.

quantity of bright red hair – usually topped by a man's Homburg hat – and her booming voice. She fell out with many people, including Sir George Chetwynd who at one time managed her horses at Bedford Lodge. When the Duchess announced that she wanted Sir George to remove his horses as she intended to make Bedford Lodge a private stable for Craw and herself, Sir George left, but took the trainer as well. As a result the Duchess and her husband were forced to move to a stable across the Bury Road in Newmarket which she named Sefton Lodge after Craw's Derby winner. Sadly he died shortly after the move, when they were both in the South of France. (It may have been the occasion when, in the middle of a heated argument in the casino at Monto Carlo, the Duchess drew herself up and demanded, 'Do you realize I am the Duchess of Montrose.' She could not have expected the answering report, 'Are you really, from your language I should have taken you for the Duchess of Billingsgate.')

The Duchess had been very fond of Craw and brought his body back to England. It was buried next door to St Agnes's church, which she built in his memory beside the stables at Sefton Lodge. Present-day vicars can rest assured that they will not suffer the fate of the Duchess's long-standing incumbent, the Reverend Colville Wallis. On one occasion he was insensitive enough to pray for fine weather to assist the harvest after a very wet summer. What he did not know was that the Duchess had a horse running in the St Leger, which was particularly suited to wet ground. It was too much for Her Grace. In the middle of the service she got up and stormed out, to confront the poor Wallis afterwards: 'How dare you pray for fine weather in my church when you know it will ruin my horse's chances. I shall not allow you to preach in my church again!' Fortunately Wallis knew the Duchess well by this time and, after profuse apologies, the storm blew over and he stayed for many years.

The greatest *bête-noirs* of the Duchess's life were handicappers, who she viewed to a man with deep suspicion and often accused them of unfairly handicapping her horses. She constantly referred to one of their number with an unfortunately ugly face as, 'the man who murdered his mother'. Major Egerton, another handicapper, must have been somewhat surprised when she once accused him: 'I see from the way you handicap my horses you are desirous of riding them yourself. I only intend to say that on no account will you be gratified.' She kept up a long-running rivalry with Captain Machell who was for many years her nearest neighbour at Bedford Cottage. Although it was mainly friendly rivalry the Duchess did once rather unfairly accuse the Captain of having run over her favourite dog on purpose, maintaining that he did so one evening when driving home drunk.

After Stirling Crawfurd's death the Duchess continued to run his horses as well as her own in his apt scarlet colours. But no one expected her to marry again, which she did when aged seventy. Her third husband, Henry Milner, was twenty-four. To the end of her life the Duchess was as combative as ever and addressed most people as though they were one of her jockeys. The dispersal sale of her horses after her death in 1894 revealed the quality of the animals she and Crawfurd had consistently bred and owned: in addition to Canterbury Pilgrim, her mother Pilgrimage was sold carrying a foal called Jeddah who won the Derby in 1898. Despite her contentiousness the Duchess was greatly missed in Newmarket, for 'Old Six Mile Bottom' as she was sometimes disrespectfully referred to, had become a figure of considerable affection to the racing fraternity.

The only other lady who indulged extensively in a career as an owner during the period was someone who throughout her life rarely felt bound by any conventions or rules – Lillie Langtry. When she first arrived in England from her native Jersey – where she had already given an inkling of her priorities in life by marrying Edward Langtry because he had a large yacht – Lillie Langtry was preoccupied with ensuring her social advancement.

As most of her admirers and lovers, not least the Prince of Wales, were all actively involved in racing, and given her own penchant for a gamble, it was inevitable that Lillie would be drawn to racing. It was while staying with

A tense moment.

Ferdinand de Rothschild for Goodwood races that she had a lucky escape when her dress went up in flames while her maid was lighting the bedroom fire. Sir George Chetwynd, who came to blows over her with Lord Lonsdale, took the trouble to advise her about betting in an attempt to help her avoid getting into hopeless debt: 'Make out your account every night after a day's racing . . . never let your account be missing at Tattersall's . . .' It seems his advice was necessary. A contemporary journalist recalled seeing her lay £100 on a horse which he could have told her would run like a pig.

It was not until the advent of her infamous affair with the Squire, George Alexander Baird, that Lillie Langtry became an owner. Previously she had not been able to afford it, but as well as the huge sums of money that he showered upon her – normally to atone for his physical abuse of her – the Squire also gave her her first horses. The two met at Newmarket races and their notoriety was mutually fascinating. After Baird had strongly advised her to back two of his horses, both of which subsequently won, Lillie agreed to dine with him after the races. Thus began the most turbulent – if lucrative – two years of her life. In many ways Baird was a most unlikely choice for Lillie Langtry, for, despite her reputation, her choice of men had undoubtedly shown a discerning – not to say avaricious – eye. (It was a mark of her achievement that Princess Alexandra was happier to receive Lillie Langtry than the indisputably aristocratic successor to her husband's favours, Daisy Brooke.)

In 1892 Baird gave Lillie a two-year-old called Milford, a horse of outstanding quality by Saraband who had been a top-class contemporary of the illustrious Ormonde, Minting and The Bard. Racing in her own turquoise and fawn colours, under the assumed name of 'Mr Jersey' which left little doubt as to the identity of the owner as she was widely known as 'the Jersey Lily', Milford gave Lillie Langtry her first win in the Coventry Stakes at Royal Ascot. His owner was ecstatic and began to entertain visions of herself as the first woman to own the winner of the Derby. As a result she turned down an offer of £20,000 immediately after the race, a huge sum considering that at that time no one had payed more that 5000 guineas for a yearling. She was later bitterly to regret the decision, but when Milford won the July Stakes at Newmarket a few weeks later, she seemed on the verge of as glittering a career as an owner as she had enjoyed as a courtesan. It was not to be. The next year Baird died in America and Lillie nearly lost Milford completely. Baird's trustees could find no deed of gift relating to the horse and therefore demanded that she return him to be sold with Baird's other animals. Already incensed by being left nothing in Baird's will, Lillie refused outright to consent

The boots Lillie wore to the races.

to the final ignominy. She was successful in her refusal thanks to the inevitable intervention of George Lewis in the nick of time. Milford went on to win ten more races – but their value was nothing approaching £20,000 and he was a failure at stud.

Lillie Langtry: successful courtesan and owner.

In 1896 Lillie Langtry paid 1600 guineas for Merman, an Australian four-year-old, who was to bring her greatest success as an owner – and a gambler. The next year he won the Cesarewitch at odds of 8 to 1 and Lillie collected a huge sum. Ironically, she heard a few days later that her husband, the wretched Edward Langtry, had died in an asylum in Chester, having been picked up as a vagrant and alcoholic. Two years later, on the day that Merman won the Goodwood Cup which he followed up with the Goodwood Plate, Lillie Langtry married Hugo de Bathe, the son of a baronet. It was widely reckoned that Hugo's father disinherited him immediately. It is unlikely that it would have worried the young man's new wife; her husband was undeniably good-looking and she would soon be Lady de Bathe.

As Lady de Bathe she went on to win the Cesarewitch a second time in 1908 with Yentoi. And although she no longer enjoyed with Edward VII the intimacy of the old days, it seemed they were still friends and that he valued her opinion. Around the time that Minoru won the Derby for the King, it was widely rumoured that he intended to take his horses away from Richard Marsh at Egerton House, as he had been influenced to believe that Egerton was too expensive. At the time Lillie had her private stables and a small house at Ethelreda House, in a village near to Newmarket. Meeting her at the sale paddocks in Newmarket, Marsh asked whether she might be able to intervene on his behalf. Following a visit by the King to Ethelreda shortly afterwards she was able to inform Marsh – as the King was on his way to see Minoru – that he would be staying at Egerton. Unfortunately Minoru decided to misbehave that day and although he had made up his mind the King could not resist saying petulantly to his trainer: 'I suppose we shall have to stay at Egerton, but there will be sheep on the lawns and only ten horses in training!' As for Lady de Bathe, she did not die until 1929, in somewhat reduced circumstances. Shortly before her death she wrote wistfully: 'In life I have had all that I really wanted very much – a yacht, a racing stable, a theatre of my own, lovely gardens . . .'

BLACK ASCOT

Leopold de Rothschild ignores the rain as he leads in St Amant, his 1904 Derby winner.

King Edward VII was sixty when – at last – he ascended to the throne in 1901. He devoted himself to his tasks as the monarch with an energy and commitment which surprised some people. But if he was content to make radical alterations in the way that he spent much of his time, he had absolutely no intention of changing either the way of life he had been perfecting for decades, or the type of people who surrounded him. No one, not even his mother, had been allowed to influence his choice of friends. Now that he was King he was certainly not going to heed the criticisms of members of the old guard, such as Lady Paget, who had been a member of Queen Victoria's Court. 'The King as King, is more useful than he was as Prince of Wales. He has a great deal of ability, but is always surrounded by a bevy of Jews and a ring of racing people. He has the same luxuriant tastes of the Semites, the same love of pleasure and comfort.' The crusty old lady did, however, condescend to add, 'Still, he is a *charmeur* and very able.'

If anything, the Semites that Lady Paget referred to with distaste, were on the ascendant; at least on the Turf. In 1911, when Jack Joel's horse Sunstar won the Derby, there were so many runners with Jewish owners that one

onlooker was heard to remark, 'We ought to thank God for the Jews or there'd be no Derby this year.' Jack Joel and his brother Solly were sons of an East End publican. Following their uncle, Barney Barnato, to South Africa, they took over the enormous diamond empire he had built up and established a virtual monopoly of the whole trade. When they embarked on their racing careers in England in the late 1890s, they both became leading patrons of the Turf and continued to be so into the inter-war years. Sunstar's was the first of three Derby's and a number of other Classics they won between them. It was not only the sport which drew the Joel brothers to racing; the huge party which Solly gave at Maiden Erleigh, his home near Reading, every year on the Sunday before Ascot week, became one of the best-known events of the royal meeting.

The Joel brothers were representative – if wealthier than most – of those men who had made millions abroad and returned to England to spend their money establishing a lifestyle of luxurious comfort. At the same time the beneficiaries of fortunes amassed at home – such as Harry McCalmont – held similar ambitions. It seemed that the death of Queen Victoria, as well as the dawning of a new century, had lifted the last limitations imposed by the old code of Victorianism. The result was a period of unparalleled spending as people no longer appeared to be reticent about flaunting their wealth. Money began to prove it could bring as much power as land and, if dispensed in the right way, social acceptance.

Racing was one of the main beneficiaries. Consumed with frustrated anger and astonishment, one Liberal politician complained that more money was spent on hunting, shooting and – in particular – racing, than on the whole of the British navy. The social importance of racing was given a new impetus by the fact that Edward VII was now King and people were quick to appreciate the potential benefits of involving themselves as owners, or as hosts for one or more of the main meetings. When William Dodge James, the heir to an American industrial fortune was looking for a house in England one reason that he chose West Dean Park in Sussex was its proximity to Goodwood. West Dean became one of the bastions of Edwardian country-house life. As well as the entertainment of a large house party for a racing weekend it benefitted from the novelties which were making life for the moneyed élite not only enjoyable, but increasingly modern and comfortable: motor cars instead of carriages, central heating and telephones.

The old-established landed families might violently disapprove of the plutocrats who were forcing their way into Society by virtue of newly made fortunes, but by the early 1900s they had to accept that the newcomers were

Diamond king: Jack Joel raises his hat to a friend at Goodwood.

Lord Howard de Walden:
as much an aesthete as a sportsman.

Bob Sievier and his wonderful mare
Sceptre, who won four Classics.

there to stay. Many of them showed an equal ability to spend. One of Lord Derby's first actions after he inherited in 1908 was to sell Derby House in St James's Square and buy a larger house in Stratford Place, which he renamed Derby House. When asked why he had bought it he replied calmly, 'Lady Derby must have somewhere to change when she comes up from Coworth to go to the theatre.' Derby was known as 'the King of Lancashire' and the stud which he built up at Knowsley was on a similar scale to the palatial Stanley House stable in Newmarket. As for the vast house at Knowsley, the household bills were rarely less than £50,000 per annum in the years leading up to the First World War.

There were many new faces among the leading owners at the turn of the century, including Lord Howard de Walden, an immensely rich young man who had inherited in 1899 at the age of nineteen. His son, the present Lord Howard de Walden, explained the family's fortune somewhat modestly when he attributed it to one of those convenient marriages when the bride brought with her a few farms on the edge of London. Those farms are now a substantial area just north of Oxford Street.

Lord Howard de Walden was able to establish himself as a leading owner almost immediately by purchasing all of Harry McCalmont's horses after the Colonel's death. All, that is, except the great Isinglass, who was retained by the McCalmont family at stud at Cheveley Park. Among the horses was a son of Persimmon called Zinfandel who was prevented from running as a three-year-old – thus missing the chance to win the Derby – by the death of his late owner. He soon established himself as a four-year-old in 1904 by winning the Coronation Cup when he beat Rock Sand, who had won the Triple Crown the year before and Sceptre who had won four Classics in 1902.

Lord Howard de Walden was one of the few patrons of the Turf to have any real contact with the intellectuals and artists of the time. He himself wrote a number of plays and was often seen dipping into a pocket-sized edition of his favourite verse at race meetings. His distinctive and rather aesthetic apricot racing colours were suggested by his friend, Augustus John and a number of his racing contemporaries found it hard to equate his enjoyment of racing with his more rarified, academic pursuits.

In direct contrast to the retiring Lord Howard de Walden was Robert Standish Sievier, who rocketed into the headlines as an owner in the early years of the century. Opinions of Bob Sievier varied as to whether he was a likeable rogue or a disreputable crook. He was well known as a heavy punter and through the season of 1900 won an enormous amount of money – including £53,000 at the Epsom meeting alone. When the recently deceased

Duke of Westminster's yearlings came up for sale at the end of the year Sievier seized the opportunity to invest his newly won fortune. Among the yearlings was a filly called Sceptre, a daughter of Persimmon, which Sievier had seen and was determined to buy. The evening before the sale he went to Mr Somerville Tattersall, who was conducting the sale, and to Tattersall's considerable alarm as the banks were closed for the night, deposited £20,000 in cash with him as security for the bids he would make the next day. Sievier got Sceptre for £10,000 – easily a record price for a yearling. He spent most of the rest of his £20,000 on a selection of the other Westminster yearlings.

Confident though he was of Sceptre's potential, Sievier could not have imagined quite how successful she would be. As a three-year-old in 1902 she won all the Classics except the Derby and a total of £25,650 in prize money. Sievier became the first man to win four out of the five Classics in a season and headed the list of winning owners. He was also training his own horses, having sacked his American trainer at the beginning of the season. It was this which led his enemies to maintain that the remarkable filly never reached her full potential and that if the Duke of Westminster had been alive and she had been trained by John Porter she would have made a clean sweep of the Classics.

Despite Sceptre's victories, Sievier was forced by financial problems to sell her at the beginning of the next season. She was bought by the brewing magnate Sir William Bass, for £25,000 and went on to win a further £12,500 for her new owner. Whatever Sievier's enemies said, there was no doubt that Sceptre was a superb racehorse and, with Pretty Polly, owned by Colonel

Motor cars made transport to the races faster, but no less elegant.

Pretty Polly parading before she won the Oaks in 1904.

Black Ascot: the Royal enclosure only half full and the Royal Box empty.

Loader, who won three Classics in 1904, one of a distinguished pair of the greatest race mares of all time.

For Sievier himself, the tide of success continued to ebb. In 1904, after losing a slander action in court he was warned off by the Stewards of the Jockey Club. Not long afterwards Jack Joel took out a blackmail charge against him, although in the event Sievier was found not guilty. Banned from active involvement in racing, he turned to sporting journalism and started his own paper, *The Winning Post* which soon enjoyed considerable success. It was, however, a very different story from the days of Sceptre's triumphs.

One name which hardly figured in the lists of winning owners during the early years of his reign was that of racing's dominant figure, King Edward VII. In 1900, the year of Diamond Jubilee's Triple Crown, he had won a total of nearly £30,000 in prize-money. Throughout the seven years following his total was only just more than half that amount. It was largely as a result of his shortage of good horses that, in 1907, Lord Marcus Beresford arranged to lease some yearlings from Colonel Hall Walker who owned the Tully Stud, in Ireland. (During the First World War Colonel Hall Walker was to hand over his stud to the Government as the foundation of what became the National Stud.) Among the horses leased by the King was a colt called Minoru which, in 1909, brought Edward VII his third victory in the Derby. It was the only time in history that the race has been won by the reigning monarch and Minoru's victory was given an even more tumultuous reception than those afforded Persimmon and Diamond Jubilee. As the King led in Minoru the crowd of thousands up and down the course broke into singing 'God Save the King'. Few of them would have guessed that less than a year later the King would be dead. It was the perfect ending that he should have gained victory in the last Derby of his lifetime.

Even during his dying hours one of the King's final pleasures came from the victory of one of his horses. On 6 May 1910 his filly Witch of the Air was entered for a two-year-old race at Kempton Park. The day before a bulletin from Buckingham Palace had announced that the King's condition 'causes some anxiety'. As a result Richard Marsh went to the Palace on his way through London from Newmarket to Kempton to ask after the King and whether, in the circumstances, the filly should run. He was given the message that the King had ordered that she should. The race was at 4.15 p.m. and Witch of the Air's win was telegraphed straight to Buckingham Palace. When the future King George V congratulated his father the King replied, 'Yes, I have heard of it. I am very glad'. He died that evening.

The King's death shocked the nation for few people had known that he

was ill. Margot Asquith whose husband by this time was the Liberal Prime Minister, wrote in her diary the day after the King's death that Sir Ernest Cassel (the millionaire Jewish financier and close friend of Edward VII's) came to see her and they sat together on a sofa and wept. Of all the tributes which appeared after the King's death none would have moved him more than the spectacle of Royal Ascot six weeks later. *The Times* edition of the first day carried the solemn reminder: 'Lord Churchill wishes to remind ladies and gentlemen attending Ascot Races in the Royal Enclosure that they should wear black, as the period of full mourning is not yet expired.' Forever after the meeting was known as 'Black Ascot' and the scene was one of overpowering sombreness. Ladies were dressed in black from head to foot and men wore tall hats with mourning bands. The only breaks in the ranks of dark colour were the occasional bunches of flowers pinned to ladies' dresses. The race-cards were all edged with black, the Royal Stand closed and the blinds of the Royal Box drawn. For four days Society and the racing world remembered a King who had been such a dominant personality on the Turf.

Despite the gloom it was soon clear that Edward VII's racing interests were to be maintained and all his horses were bequeathed to King George V. Soon after the King's death Richard Marsh heard from Sir Dighton Probyn, whose attitude to the royal racing interests had changed somewhat since the time when he warned John Porter that he would, 'ruin the Prince of Wales if he continued to buy thoroughbreds.' Sir Dighton wrote:

Derby disaster: the suffragette Emily Davison is fatally injured as she runs in front of the King's horse, Anmer, in 1913.

I heartily congratulate you, and our young King also, that he proposes carrying on King Edward's racing establishments at Newmarket and Sandringham, in the same way as his great father did ... I trust that King George may long go on racing with you as his trainer, and that Sandringham may produce of the same type of animals it did during our late dear King's time. I know you will give me a tip of any good ones when you think you have them as, although I have nothing to do with the stud now, I take, and for ever shall take, the greatest interest in it.

During the period of court mourning after Edward VII's death the royal horses were leased to Lord Derby. From when they were returned to King George V, Richard Marsh continued to train for him until 1924. George V did not enjoy his father's success on the Turf, and in 1913 one of his horses was involved in the most sensational and tragic event to occur at the Derby or on any racecourse during the period. It was at the time when the Suffragette movement was at its height and one of its most fervent members, Miss Emily Davison chose Derby Day to make a dramatic demonstration. The King had a horse called Anmer running and as the field rounded Tattenham Corner, Emily Davison rushed out from the crowd and attempted to catch hold of the horse's bridle. She, the horse and jockey – Herbert Jones – were all thrown to the ground and although both the horse and rider were unharmed Miss Davison suffered a fractured skull and died four days later without recovering consciousness. Her action overshadowed the other extraordinary aspect of the race in which the winner, Craganour, was disqualified and the race awarded to a 100 to 1 outsider, Aboyeur. Queen Alexandra showed her displeasure in a forthright cable to Herbert Jones, Anmer's jockey: 'Queen Alexandra was very sorry indeed to hear of your sad accident caused through the abominable behaviour of a brutal, lunatic woman. I telegraph now by Her Majesty's command to enquire how you are getting on and to express Her Majesty's sincere hope that you may soon be alright again! Dighton Probyn.

It was a tragic manner in which to end the period, but at the same time an outward sign of the unrest which was developing and would shatter the halcyon stability of Edwardian society. Never again would there be the abundant leisure time and affluence among the upper classes which had been the prerequisites of their life for four decades and which enabled them to indulge in racing on such a scale. Racing provided the answers to most of the Edwardians' loves and priorities: the ability to spend money and gamble, beautiful horses and fashionable women, excitement and gossip, the excuse for a house party, and, most important, royal patronage. The appetite – and the opportunities – for their way of life was largely destroyed by the First World War and, like the other pastimes they had enjoyed, racing changed accordingly and forever.

The last Derby, 1909. Edward VII waits with delight to lead in Minoru after becoming the first — and only — monarch to own the Derby winner. A year later he was dead.

BIBLIOGRAPHY

Asquith, M. *Autobiography*. (Thornton Butterworth Ltd. 1920).

Astley, Sir J. *Fifty Years of My Life*. (Hurst and Blackett Ltd. 1894).

Booth, J. B. *Old Pink 'Un Days*. (Grant Richards Ltd. 1924).

Booth, J. B. *Sporting Times*. (Grant Richards Ltd. 1938).

Brough, J. *The Prince and the Lily*. (Hodder and Stoughton. 1975).

Cawthorne, G. J. and Herod, R. S. *Royal Ascot*. (Longmans, Green and Co. 1900).

Chetwynd, Sir G. *Racing Reminiscenses*. (Longmans, Green and Co. 1891).

Churchill, W. S. *Lord Randolph Churchill*. (Macmillan. 1906).

Cornwallis-West, G. *Edwardian Hey-Days*. (Putnam. 1930).

Cowles, V. *King Edward VII and his Circle*. (Hamish Hamilton. 1956).

Crewe, Marquess of. *Lord Rosebery*. (John Murray. 1931).

Fairfax-Blackborough, J. *The Analysis of the Turf*. (Philip Allan and Co. 1927).

Fane, Lady A. *Chit Chat*. (Thornton Butterworth Ltd. 1926).

Havers, Sir M and others. *The Royal Baccarat Scandal*. (William Kimber. 1977).

Joel, S. *Ace of Diamonds*. (Frederick Muller Ltd. 1958).

Lambton, the Hon G. *Men and Horses I Have Known*. (Thornton Butterworth Ltd. 1924).

Lang, T. *My Darling Daisy*. (Michael Joseph. 1966).

Leach, H. *The Duke of Devonshire*. (Methuen. 1904).

Londonderry, Marchioness of. *Henry Chaplin*. (Macmillan and Co. 1926).

Longrigg, R. *The History of Horseracing*. (Macmillan and Co. 1972).

Marsh, R. *Trainer to Two Kings*. (Cassell and Co. 1925).

Mortimer, R. *The Jockey Club*. (Cassell and Co. 1958).

Morton, C. *My Sixty Years On the Turf*. (Hutchinson. 1930).

Nevill, R. *The Sport of Kings*. (Methuen. 1926).

Onslow, R. *Headquarters*. (Great Ouse Press. 1983).

Onslow, R. *The Squire*; (Harrap. 1980)

Pless, Princess Daisy of. *What I Left Unsaid*. (Cassell and Co. 1936).

Porter, J. *John Porter of Kingsclere*. (Grant Richards Ltd. 1919).

Portland, Duke of. *Memories of Racing and Hunting*. (Faber and Faber. 1935).

Portland, Duke of. *Men, Women and Things*. (Faber and Faber. 1937).

Roby, K. *The King, the Press and the People*. (Barrie and Jenkins. 1975).

Rossmore, Lord. *Things I Can Tell*. (Eveleigh Nash. 1912).

St Aubyn, G. *Edward VII: Prince and King*. (Atheneum. 1979).

Seth-Smith, M. *A Classic Connexion*. (Secker and Warburg. 1983).
Sutherland, D. *The Yellow Earl*. (Cassell and Co. 1965)
Sykes, C. *The Visitors' Book*. (Weidenfeld and Nicolson. 1978).
Thormanby, W. *Kings of the Turf*. (Hutchinson and Co. 1898).
Watson, A. E. T. *King Edward VII as a Sportsman*. (Longmans, Green and Co. 1911).
Watson, A. E. T. *The Turf*. (Longmans, Green and Co. 1898).
Warwick, Countess of. *Afterthoughts*. (Cassell and Co. 1931).

INDEX